fresh
happy
tasty

DVF studio

Happy Eating to you!
Love Jane.

fresh
happy
tasty

An Adventure in
100 Recipes

Jane Coxwell

Photographs by John Bedell

wm WILLIAM MORROW *An Imprint of* HarperCollins*Publishers*

FRESH HAPPY TASTY. Copyright © 2013 by Jane Coxwell. All rights reserved. Printed in the United States of America. No part of this book may be used or reproduced in any manner whatsoever without written permission except in the case of brief quotations embodied in critical articles and reviews. For information address HarperCollins Publishers, 10 East 53rd Street, New York, NY 10022.

HarperCollins books may be purchased for educational, business, or sales promotional use. For information please write: Special Markets Department, HarperCollins Publishers, 10 East 53rd Street, New York, NY 10022.

FIRST EDITION

Designed by Lorie Pagnozzi

Food photography by John Bedell

Travel photography by Jane Coxwell; travel photographs featuring Jane taken by crew members or passersby

Library of Congress Cataloging-in-Publication Data has been applied for.

ISBN 978-0-06-212540-8

13 14 15 16 17 [DIX/RRD] 10 9 8 7 6 5 4 3 2 1

To my parents - thank you for everything. x

contents

foreword

When Jane came to *Eos* as a chef, we all immediately fell in love with her food! It is exactly the kind of food that I love: simple, fresh, and incredibly tasty. Jane is a magician. It is truly magical how she chooses ingredients and brings out their supreme flavor by introducing the right herbs and spices. Her food is healthy, colorful, tasty, and provocative. It is never too heavy, often surprising, and very easy to understand. Like Jane herself, her food is inviting and not intimidating. It is spectacular, special food for every day. It is about embracing the experience of enjoying your taste buds and giving eating simply a whole new meaning. It is about sharing and loving.

I was so inspired by Jane and her unique approach to food that I suggested she write this book. I love the way she improvises, experiments, and surprises the taste buds. I love the way she presents her creations. I love the lack of pretention and the simplicity. I love the generosity of it all!

Jane is the best cook I ever met; and I am glad that you can all invite her into your kitchen, share her secrets, and enjoy!

Love,
Diane von Furstenberg

Introduction

Growing up in Cape Town, South Africa, I didn't have dreams of becoming a chef. Some chefs have great stories of standing on chairs in the kitchen while they made Bolognese sauce with their Italian grandmothers, but I don't.

While other future chefs were baking their first banana breads, I was skateboarding with my best friend, Luke, while wearing my favorite Bart Simpson T-shirt. Or collecting friends' tennis balls from the storm drains under the street we lived on (earning me the name Jane-the-drain with neighbors). Honestly, I found mealtimes to be a bit of a chore, and I'd try to hide my unfinished food under my knife and fork before saying the mandatory "May I please be excused from the table" as I put my crisp, white, unused napkin back into its ring, so that I could be outdoors again, riding my bike.

Looking back, though, I realize that I did grow up around a table. My parents always have been hugely sociable, and still are—we always had people over for dinner. When I was very little, one of my favorite things was to crawl under the dining room table and fall asleep listening to the many people above talking, laughing, and sharing food.

It's still actually one of my favorite things to do, and people who know me really well know that after a meal I might disappear to a couch close by and fall asleep (although I haven't admitted up until now that I'm actually sleeping) while they're still sitting around the table, laughing and being merry.

Looking back, these experiences had a major effect on the type of career I fell into and, more important, the type of food I make today. While my love of food itself is very pure, I do feel that somehow I was groomed to see it as a way of connecting. Food is so important in our everyday lives—it keeps us together.

The food I like to make facilitates this togetherness. Whether it's for a special occasion or day-to-day living, it's the string that ties experiences together. We need to eat to survive, of course, but the gift we've been given—to make food delicious, fun, nourishing, and celebratory—is amazing. And we should make the most of it!

I moved to London straight after I finished high school, itching to see the world and have new experiences. I lived there for a couple of very happy years, traveling when I could and working very hard at strange jobs (such as selling alarm systems door-to-door through two English winters, meeting some pretty incredible—and incredibly odd—people in their homes along the way).

I felt as if I needed to choose a career, though, so I moved back to South Africa to ponder my options. A friend was just about to attend culinary school to study under one of South Africa's very best chefs, David Higgs, and one night I was hanging out and looking through his files when he told me that one of the other students had just dropped out. A feeling hit me—*I have to do this*—even though I'd never even scrambled an egg. Classes were starting in five days, so I pulled myself together, went to see the chef really early the next morning, and persuaded him to take me. I told him I'd work harder than any of the other students to get to the top of the class. I was honestly really lucky to get in.

That feeling was right: From that first day at school, I fell head over heels in love with food and cooking. It was all new to me, and I was fully conscious as I dove into the experience. Every ingredient I was introduced to (which, let's be honest, was everything) was a total marvel. I remember opening my first peapod and being completely in awe of the "packaging." Even consciously seasoning a dish for the first time was a total eye-opener in that I suddenly understood what seasoning was and how important it is. It was amazing to learn about the versatility of the simple egg, and the little powers it holds, from lifting an airy cake to purifying a soup.

I decided to pursue a role that would expand my new romance with food. I wanted to do it all—go to food markets, plan the menus, cook the food and plate it, and know my guests and make it personal to them. So that's what I did. A short time after I finished culinary school, I made my way to the South of France. Arriving with 200 euros and a book called *How to Work on Yachts and Superyachts,* I knew no one but found a hostel to stay in that had fake plastic grass, campers, and lots of young people drinking cheap wine from two-liter bottles.

Fast-forward ten years, and here I am. I've spent most of that time traveling around the world cooking for people on their private yachts, spending extensive time all over the Mediterranean, the Adriatic, and the Caribbean. I took about two years off from traveling at one point and was offered a job as head chef of a wonderful winery, Hall Wines in St. Helena in the Napa Valley. The Halls allowed me to grow and refine myself as a chef in what is basically chef heaven. I loved my time there, and learned so much from being around some of the world's best chefs. (Like one of my dear friends, Kelly, who taught me to make the most of the vineyards and took me foraging for miner's lettuce, bright yellow mustard flowers, and other little edible flowers and bitter greens. This is the finesse of Napa Valley chefs.)

But I wasn't quite finished with the traveling yet, and I was able to land myself a job on the world's most beautiful yacht, *Eos,* working for Diane von Furstenberg and Barry Diller, an incredible couple with a wonderful sense of adventure. I joined them four years ago, and we've circumnavigated the world. This position has allowed me and my fellow crewmates to discover and experience places we'd never have dreamed of otherwise; often they can be reached only by boat. Some of the places are so remote that we've been told by local chiefs that that time would be remembered as the year of *Eos*. All the while, I've been able to cook and taste and experience.

Cooking for Diane von Furstenberg has been a real joy. She's adventurous, willing to try new things, and has a really remarkable and discerning palate. The food she likes to eat matches her personality: vibrant and colorful. She's so generous in sharing with family and friends, constantly bringing people together and making every meal a moment to connect and celebrate.

She has an amazing ability to inspire everyone she comes into contact with, and she has certainly inspired me to be better all the time, and to think outside the box—not just with food but in life.

world food

I've traveled around the world cooking. What a dream!

I've eaten some crazy things and in some pretty wild places. I've had Mopane worms in Zimbabwe, bat in Vanuatu (which I also learned to cook, and then served to guests—unsuccessfully), brains in Istanbul, fish hearts at a seafood market in Indonesia, and, thinking back, a lot of things that I'm still not completely sure what they were.

When we get to a new port, I usually set off by myself with some local money, and sometimes a local guide for translation and knowledge, to find food. I go to markets, farms, kitchens, and any other place that people tell me to go to. Some of the places the boat took us to were so remote that just us being there was a local event.

However delicious or obscure the food, the thing that makes these experiences special to me is the incredible bonds formed with people all over the world.

Our languages and cultures may be worlds apart, but we connect over food almost effortlessly. I've loved every minute. Well, almost . . . sometimes it feels like *Bizarre Foods with Andrew Zimmern*—but without the camera crew or cold water bottles afterward. A lot of times it was just me in some incredibly remote place, with a proud local handing me some odd-looking thing to put in my mouth.

Think: 100 degrees outside, the smell of a fish market at 100 degrees, an old man handing you something gray and mushy wrapped in an old banana leaf, with an expectant look on his face. Then you turn around to see the whole market looking at you. You have to eat that warm (and not from the oven) gray thing. The whole thing. You must swallow it while the market watches, and then make a face to suggest you liked it, or at least found it interesting. After that, you'll just get handed more.

But that's part of the fun of it, I guess. Some places I've visited were really surprising—the South Pacific island of Vanuatu raises some wonderful beef, and my second chef, Craig, and I were taken to a beautiful shrimp farm at the foot of some mountains, where we ate raw shrimp, just pulled from the water.

When we were planning our trip to the Galápagos Islands, I made a stop in Quito, Ecuador, to try to make some food connections. I wandered the streets from market to market looking for fresh food. Only when I got to the Galápagos Islands and hit the local five a.m. Saturday market did I find food in abundance! Different food abundances, though—lobsters for $7 and chickens for $30. The fish market alone is worth a visit to the Galápagos Islands—the fishermen stand by their stalls while pelicans and seals sit at their feet waiting for scraps. Incredible!

But one of the best fish markets I've ever visited must be in Venice, Italy, with my captain, Jerry, who's seafood crazy. Jumping in a water taxi to get to the fish market in Venice should be in all the tourist guides.

Living on a boat for long periods of time means that sometimes the best seafood comes to you. In the Pacific, I used to buy my fish early in the morning from local fishermen who came up to the boat in their tiny dugout canoes. Using the bilges as a live fish tank was a great way to keep the fish fresh. Some fishermen were pretty brave—in the Solomon Islands, I bought enormous live coconut crabs from a man in the same type of tiny canoe, and those crabs can easily take off fingers and toes! In the Caribbean, I buy fish from the side of the boat too. I've been using a man called Mr. Wonderful as my fish purveyor there for years. (Last season, after some consideration, he asked me to be his wife.)

I'm so thankful for the many incredible memories and experiences these last few years on the boat have given me. I've tasted food from all over the world and learned from local experts everywhere from Singapore to Morocco. My food has taken a bit of influence from everywhere I've been, and will continue to do so. It's world food.

how to use this book

When I started cooking, I was always wondering whether I was doing things correctly. Where I'd added too much of something, or whether I could combine certain ingredients.

I'm still learning, but the freedom that has come with not being bound by recipes and rules is wonderful. I do look at cookbooks, read recipes online, and watch cooking shows—there are so many things to discover and learn—but I can't remember the last time I felt bound by someone else's recipe. In that same spirit, I'd really like *Fresh Happy Tasty* to be seen as the kind of cookbook that guides rather than instructs.

The recipes are pretty simple, and I tried to include as many photos as I could. The style of cooking is relaxed and happy, and it produces tasty food with a minimum of effort.

I don't think food should be taken too seriously, especially not everyday food. I cook for people in my everyday life, and not in a restaurant environment, so my objective is to make food delicious, healthy, comforting, and a little exciting, all in one.

It's important that you're not bound by recipes—mine or anyone else's. I don't know how juicy your lemons are, or how hot your oven or chiles are! I haven't chosen your onions, or picked out your garlic, so I don't know how big they are. I don't know whether you use gas or electric, or the last time you had your oven calibrated, so the results we get from "400°F for 20 minutes" are going to be different. I encourage you to taste, taste, taste, and be present in the cooking process. Check things in the oven and prod and poke as you're working.

I'd like to think that every ingredient won't be meticulously measured out, but that you'll get a feeling for it, and be able to use your hands and eyes to start measuring things out. This is a much more enjoyable way of cooking. When you're cooking without worrying about instructions, it's a getaway. I like to put some music on and pour myself a glass of wine (depending on the time of day!).

Be happy, have fun, love food.

A Word About Ingredients

It's not my intention to keep you reading too long,
but there are a couple of things that I wanted to mention
about certain ingredients that are fundamental in my food.

agave nectar

Agave has become a staple in my kitchen and cooking. I used to use sugar or maple syrup to finish off some dishes, but it bothered me a little that they weren't very good for you. Agave nectar is a wonderful substitute and not bad for you. It's sweeter than honey and sugar, so you need less of it. I buy the "light" one, which has a mellow flavor that blends well with most dishes. Also, I love that you can find it in a squeezy bottle—so easy to use!

garlic

I use a lot of garlic. I use it raw, which for some people is a no-no, but when prepared properly, it's great. And if it's fresh, it won't smell.

A few things:

- Never buy chopped processed garlic unless vampires are an issue with you—it will make you smell. And avoid buying peeled garlic. I believe in saving time in the kitchen, and I believe in shortcuts when they work, but peel your own garlic—it will be freshest.

- Here's a trick to help peel your garlic. Pop some garlic cloves in water (see photo) for at least 30 minutes; the skin will come right off and it won't affect the taste or quality of the garlic. Make it a habit—when you're about to start cooking, pop your garlic in a glass of water and it will be ready for you. The only time this didn't work was when I was cooking at a soup kitchen and had to peel about 6 pounds of garlic with latex gloves on, and the gloves were already slippery. It was ridiculous.

- Consider using a Microplane to prepare your garlic. It's better than a press or grinding it on a board. If you use garlic raw, as I do sometimes, using a Microplane will help it go undetected. If you see a little green stem running through the middle of a garlic clove, remove and discard it—it's bitter.

lemons

I love lemons! I use them in just about every dish. They help to cut the fattiness in a dish and make it feel fresh. But the more I've moved toward healthier cooking, the more reliant I am on that pop of citrus. It just makes everything so lively, vibrant, and clean! My mother drinks it with hot water in the morning as a cleanser, and I try to do the same most mornings.

Lemon zest is really useful as well; it helps you make use of the fruit's wonderful essential oils. For example, say you want to marinate a fish. You wouldn't put lemon on a raw fish (unless you're making ceviche), because it'll actually cook the fish—but lemon zest does the trick.

fresh herbs

I'm truly in love with fresh herbs—they make me happy to be a cook. Everything
about them is wonderful—the way they look, smell, taste, and I even love the way
they feel ... am I going too far? I don't know, but next time you pick up a bunch
of cilantro, feel how soft and delicate those leaves are. To me herbs signify *fresh
happy tasty* more than almost anything. I use them in almost all my dishes ...
and when I use them, I use a lot.

Adding certain herbs to a dish can almost take you to a different destination.

If you have a cucumber and you dress it with cilantro and mint, it will feel Asian, but if you pair it with mint and dill, it will feel slightly North African. Dill and parsley put you in the Middle East, add basil and parsley instead and you're eating salad in the Mediterranean. Most dishes don't feel finished to me unless I've added a couple of handfuls of fragrant fresh herbs. They'll take almost any dish, no matter how simple or how complex, to another level. They've made green my favorite color.

nuts

There are simple things that will make your food taste better—not fancy techniques and weird ingredients, but getting the most out of the ingredients you do use. Respect them.

I don't think there's any point in using nuts unless you toast them first. I almost think it's unfair to a nut if you judge it untoasted. Do a quick taste test—it's incredible how they change. To me a pine nut tastes of not much before it's toasted. Pop one in your mouth and concentrate on how it tastes, how it feels in your mouth. Now eat a toasted one (see below for instructions) and notice how you can actually taste the pine in the pine nut. And now concentrate on the texture—it's crunchy and crisp and almost creamy, but untoasted it was texturally uninteresting.

Almonds are pretty much the only nuts that get away with going untoasted, but even they are dramatically improved from a light toast.

To toast nuts, heat a dry skillet over medium-low heat. Add the nuts when the pan is hot and then move them around for 3 to 4 minutes, or until they're evenly browned. (Well, I say brown, but it's more like they get a beautiful tan—don't go too far!) The time varies with the type of nut, so just keep an eye on them and never, ever let them burn. If you do, throw them away. It's hard to do, but you'll ruin your whole dish if you use them.

red onions

For 99 percent of my cooking, when onions are called for I use red onions. I noticed myself reaching for them more and more, and these days I rarely pick up a white onion or shallot. I like red onions because they have a beautiful sweet flavor and they're milder than yellow or white onions. This may sound silly, but to me they're not oniony. And whether I'm on a boat or in a New York City apartment, I don't have much room for storage, so I keep things simple and buy red onions. Plus, they're gorgeous!

For an interesting finish on a salad, soak some thinly sliced onion in vinegar for 30 minutes. It becomes pickled and adds a great layer of flavor.

salt

I can't say enough about Maldon salt. Try this: Slice a garden-fresh tomato and eat one slice plain. Great. Now try it with a little Maldon salt on—it's a super-tomato! Now try it with table salt—it's a salty tomato.

I'm rarely without Maldon salt. It really makes a difference. If you can't get Maldon, try to use another type of sea salt. It's really superior. And if you can't get sea salt, no worries—but just use a little less than I've directed in the recipes (if I've given an exact salt amount) because it's a little less salty than other salts.

A word about cooking

Just a few things I wanted to share with you that I feel have helped me make better food and become more confident (in the kitchen).

using your hands

Hands are my most wonderful tool. I use my hands to mix most things, and I encourage you to do the same. They're perfect for mixing and distributing because your fingertips naturally find any lumps and bumps. And what could toss a delicate salad more gently? Hands tell you when you've tossed enough—when all the ingredients are evenly dispersed, giving you a bit of everything in every mouthful, and the dressing lightly covers it all. You never want to overtoss or be rough with a salad, and your hands tell you when you've done just enough. At that point: Stop and serve.

And hands are the best way to test for doneness in fish, poultry, and meat. Get in there!

tasting

For food to be its most delicious at the moment you serve it, the most important thing is to taste, taste, taste! An underseasoned dish is disappointing. Sometimes, if I'm not 100 percent sure whether I've seasoned a dish enough, or added as much lime, lemon, or agave as I'd like to, I put a little of what I'm cooking in a small bowl or on a spoon and season it with what I think it might need. That way I don't worry about messing up my whole dish by adding too much of something. It'll give you the confidence to go for it and season and finish dishes off properly, and by this I mean to balance them: salty-sweet-sour.

tools

I don't have a load of kitchen tools that I rely on. If I had to choose, I think I could get away with having just these items.

The one thing I find I always make sure I have is the Microplane—I use it for all my garlic and most of my ginger. It's clean, and it grates the garlic into a perfect paste.

Also, tasting spoons are key! I'm constantly tasting and checking food. I really think it makes a big difference to the end result.

For knives, I ideally use a lot of different kinds, but if I'm traveling off the boat, these are the two I make sure I have. The little serrated paring knife is awesome.

The lemon squeeze is also a staple—I use a lot of lemons and don't want to take the chance of losing some lemon seeds in a finished dish. Biting into a lemon pip is a terrible experience.

Benriner Mandoline

Microplane

lemon squeeze

tasting spoons

pestle + mortar

string

wax paper

food processor

chef's knife + paring knife

Amazing early-morning boat trip in the very rural Solomon Islands. We caught a fish. The locals were just as curious about me as I was about them. Very cool experience.

Opposite page top: Pelicans at the Galápagos fish market at sunset.

Opposite page bottom: Sleeping seal, Galápagos Islands. I fell down a slippery hill taking this photo and some locals had to make a human chain to get me back up. Embarrassing!

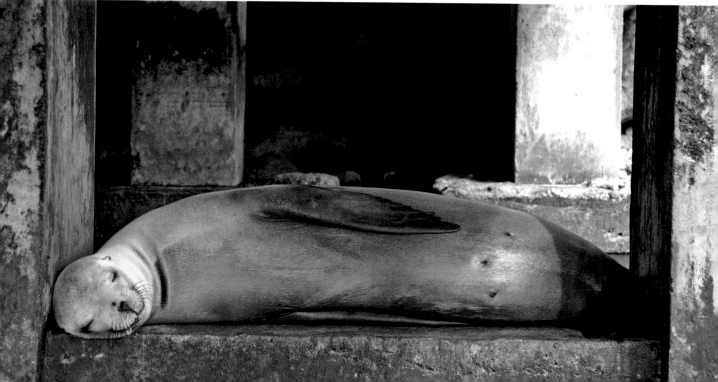

Breakfast

bircher muesli

{ Serves 2 to 4 }

This has always been a crew breakfast favorite. I love it too. It's a healthy way to start the day—in fact, it was originally created by a Swiss doctor for his patients' breakfasts. Yes, the doctor was called Dr. Bircher-Benner. Quite a revolutionary, in my eyes.

You can double this recipe for a big batch and keep it in the fridge for up to 3 days. Feel free to throw in any additional ingredients you like: banana, nuts, seeds . . .

1 cup rolled oats

1 cup apple juice

½ cup sliced almonds

1 unpeeled green apple

¼ teaspoon ground cinnamon

¼ teaspoon pure vanilla extract

½ lemon

1. In a large bowl, soak the oats in the apple juice for 30 minutes.

2. Meanwhile, toast the almonds by heating them in a small dry skillet over medium-low heat for 3 to 4 minutes, until evenly browned, stirring constantly so as not to burn them. Remove from the heat and cool.

3. Grate the apple and add it to the oats. Stir in the cinnamon, almonds, and vanilla.

4. Finish with a squeeze of lemon juice over the muesli, just enough to sharpen the flavor.

multiseed granola

{ Serves 6 }

If you have guests coming to stay, this is a massive crowd pleaser—it's lovely over plain yogurt with some fresh berries, or use it in Breakfast Verrines (page 37). Don't let the number of ingredients put you off. It's a very quick job—and once you have everything together, it's worth it!

If you aren't able to get all the ingredients, don't worry. Just use what you have, and add an even amount of any other seed, grain, sweetener, or fruit you can find.

You can keep the granola in the cupboard in a sealed container for up to a month, so you might as well make a double batch and avoid the inevitable regret when it's gone.

1½ cups whole oats

1 cup rolled oats

½ cup oat bran

½ cup wheat germ

1 cup sliced almonds

½ cup flaxseeds

½ cup poppy seeds

½ cup sesame seeds

½ cup (1 stick) unsalted butter, at room temperature

½ cup unsweetened applesauce or apple baby food

½ cup unsweetened shredded dried coconut

½ cup packed brown sugar

¼ cup maple syrup

¼ teaspoon ground cinnamon

2 teaspoons pure vanilla extract

Small pinch Maldon or other flaky salt

1. Preheat the oven to the lowest setting. Combine all the ingredients in a big bowl and use your hands to mix—it's the best way to encourage the development of lovely chunky bits in this granola. Squeeze the

mixture until the butter forms small clumps and you have clusters of a size that makes you happy.

2. Carefully pour the mixture onto a large rimmed baking sheet. Spread it into a single layer (or it won't get crispy).

3. Place the sheet in the oven and turn the temperature up to 200°F. Bake for 2 hours or until the granola is golden brown and dry, giving the sheet a careful shake a couple of times as the granola bakes.

4. Cool the granola on the sheet.

super-healthy muesli

{ Serves 10 }

This super-healthy muesli is filled with nuts, seeds, and dried fruit. If you don't have some of the ingredients, just leave them out, or add pecans and dried apricots for another great option.

Make this recipe at the same time as the Multiseed Granola (page 26) to make the most of your time and ingredients—it can be kept in a sealed container for up to a month.

I love this with almond milk, because it adds a wonderful depth and even more nutrients, but you can use any milk you like or yogurt.

2 cups rolled oats	1 cup oat bran
1 cup sliced almonds	2 teaspoons pure vanilla extract
1 cup flaxseeds	½ cup unsweetened shredded dried coconut
½ cup sesame seeds	
½ cup poppy seeds	1 cup unsweetened dried cranberries
1 cup wheat germ	1 cup dried goji berries

1. Preheat the oven to 200°F.

2. Combine all the ingredients except the dried fruit in a large bowl. Spread the mixture in a single layer onto 1 or 2 large rimmed baking sheets (take care not to overfill the trays, or the ingredients won't get crispy).

3. Bake for 1 hour, remove the sheet from the oven, and give it a shake. Increase the heat to 250°F and bake for another 30 to 40 minutes, until the nuts are very lightly toasted.

4. Let the muesli cool on the baking sheet, then toss in the dried fruit.

honey-poached pineapple

{ Serves 4 to 6 }

Poaching pineapple in honey makes it really wonderful and fragrant, like nectar. This pineapple is amazing with some tart low-fat sheep's milk yogurt and a bit of granola. Add a mint leaf, and it's heaven.

I make this ahead of time and keep it in its poaching liquid in the fridge for up to 5 days. The flavors will actually become even deeper the more time it has in the poaching liquid.

5 ounces (½ cup plus 2 tablespoons) good-quality honey

1 cinnamon stick

½ vanilla bean, split lengthwise and seeds scraped out

Zest of ¼ orange

½ large pineapple, cut into about ¾-inch cubes

Fresh mint leaves, for garnish, optional

1. In a medium saucepan over medium-high heat, bring the honey and 1 cup of water to a boil. Add the cinnamon, vanilla bean and seeds, and orange zest.

2. Reduce the heat to low and add the pineapple, stirring to combine. Tear a sheet of wax paper that's about the size of the pan and crumble it into a ball, as though you're going to throw it away. Unfurl the paper and place it in the saucepan over the pineapple. This is a great little way to stop too much liquid from evaporating.

3. Cook the pineapple for 12 to 15 minutes, checking on it every so often, making sure the simmer isn't too aggressive. When the pineapple feels fork tender and it looks as though all of the pieces have soaked up the poaching liquid (you'll see by the way it has changed color

and texture), then turn the heat off. Remove the cinnamon stick and set the pan aside to cool.

4. Serve the pineapple warm or store it in the fridge.

vanilla bean berries

{ Serves 4 }

These poached berries are a wonderful treat, especially served over Super-Healthy Muesli (page 29). This recipe is terrific for overnight guests, as it will last in the fridge for up to 5 days. On the boat, I like to poach a load of fruit at the beginning of a trip and put some out every morning. When it's been difficult to get beautiful berries transported to me, I've used frozen. Feel free to do the same—the quality of frozen berries sometimes is better than the fresh ones you'll find in the supermarket, and a lot less expensive. Just go for the best brand.

¾ cup sugar

1 vanilla bean, split lengthwise and seeds scraped out

1 cinnamon stick

Orange zest

14 ounces (2 cups) mixed berries, such as blackberries, blueberries, and raspberries

½ lemon

1. In a medium saucepan over medium-high heat, bring the sugar and 1¼ cups water to boil, stirring to dissolve the sugar.

2. Add the vanilla bean and seeds, cinnamon, and a few scrapes of orange zest. Gently simmer for about 5 minutes.

3. Stir in the berries and simmer for 1 minute, then remove from the heat and cover. Let the berries cool in the pot. Finish with a squeeze of lemon.

warm quinoa breakfast porridge

{ Serves 4 }

Almonds, quinoa, and antioxidant-rich fruit make this just about the healthiest way to start the day. This can actually be served warm in the winter months, or cold in summer months, or vice versa—whatever makes you happy!

½ cup sliced almonds

1 cup white quinoa

½ cup almond milk or low-fat cow's milk

2 tablespoons almond butter or peanut butter (smooth or chunky)

1 teaspoon honey

½ teaspoon pure vanilla extract

1 cup strawberries, hulled and quartered

1 cup raspberries

1 cup blueberries

1 handful pomegranate seeds

½ lime or lemon

A few fresh mint leaves, for garnish if desired

1. Toast the almonds as directed on page 14.

2. Bring a pot of water to a boil over medium heat and add the quinoa. Cook for about 10 minutes, until it's just underdone. Drain the quinoa and put it back in the pot over low heat.

3. Add the almond milk, almond butter, honey, and vanilla. Stir to keep the mixture moving for a couple of minutes.

4. Remove from the heat and add the berries, pomegranate seeds, and almonds. Give it a taste. If you'd like to add more honey, almond milk, fruit, or anything else, it's up to you.

5. Finish with a little squeeze of lime or lemon juice to sharpen the flavors. Serve in a bowl topped with fresh mint leaves. Beautiful.

tropical bircher muesli

{ Serves 6 }

This tropical variation on the classic Bircher Muesli tastes great in the summer.

1 cup rolled oats

¼ to ½ cup coconut water or pineapple juice

½ cup pine nuts

1 very juicy passion fruit

1 cup crushed pineapple

Flesh of 1 mango, diced

Flesh of ½ papaya, diced

¼ teaspoon pure vanilla extract

½ lime

1. Soak the oats in the coconut water for about 30 minutes.

2. Meanwhile, toast the pine nuts by heating them in a small dry skillet over medium-low heat for 3 to 4 minutes, until evenly browned. Remove from the heat and set aside.

3. To prepare the passion fruit, cut it in half, and using a spoon, scoop out the pulp and juice and stir them into the soaked oats, along with the pineapple, diced mango and papaya, pine nuts, and vanilla. Finish with a squeeze of lime.

breakfast verrines

This is more an idea than a recipe, but I wanted to include it because it's one of those things that's so simple but will make a lot of people happy.

I put these verrines out with breakfast and just let people help themselves. They would be lovely if you were hosting a brunch too. They can be made up to 2 to 3 hours in advance—if you're going to do that, sprinkle a little more granola or something crunchy on top just before you serve so that there's some texture.

I've used jars here, but glasses work just as well. Feel free to layer them with whatever you like. Here I used a combination of poached fruits, granola, and yogurt, and I've layered them in the little jars. Sometimes I use fresh fruit, such as chopped strawberries or other fresh berries. Layer them with muesli and flavored yogurts. You could add some nuts too. I've used my own granola recipe here, but you can use a good store-bought one.

A little tip for when you're making them—keep it clean. When you're layering the items in the jar or glass, wipe any smears you make on the side of the glass as you go; otherwise, it has the potential to look messy. You want to keep this dish looking clean and fresh.

rhubarb poached with vanilla bean, ginger, and cardamom

{ Serves 2 }

Often on vacation, Diane von Furstenberg will eat this poached rhubarb with sheep's milk yogurt for breakfast.

Rather than processed sugar, the poaching liquid is made from agave nectar, a natural sweetener from the blue agave plant, which is very similar to aloe vera.

1½ cups agave nectar

1 vanilla bean, split lengthwise and seeds scraped out

One ¼-inch piece fresh ginger, peeled

1 cardamom pod

Thin strips lemon zest, each about the length of half a finger

½ pound rhubarb stalks, cut into 4-inch pieces

Sheep's milk or other plain yogurt, for serving, optional

1. Combine the agave nectar, vanilla bean and seeds, ginger, cardamom, and lemon zest in a medium saucepan with 4 cups water and bring to a boil over medium-high heat. Immediately reduce the heat to low and simmer for 10 minutes.

2. Add the rhubarb and simmer for 3 to 5 minutes, until tender, depending on the size of the rhubarb. Be careful not to overcook or boil, or the rhubarb will lose its shape and fall apart.

3. Remove the pan from the heat and set aside to cool. It's ready to eat! (I leave the ginger and vanilla bean in because they look pretty, but you don't eat them.)

NOTE: *The flavors will really develop if you store it in the fridge overnight.*

best breakfast eggs

{ Serves 2 }

This is my favorite way to eat eggs in the morning. It feels fresh and clean, and it's full of flavor.

1 tablespoon extra virgin olive oil

½ cup finely chopped red onion

½ to 1 Fresno chile, seeded and finely chopped

4 eggs

2 tomatoes, seeded and chopped

Maldon or other flaky salt

Freshly ground black pepper

1 lime

1 small handful fresh cilantro leaves, roughly chopped

1 large or 2 small pita breads, toasted

1. In a medium sauté pan, heat the olive oil over low heat. Add the onion and chile and sauté for about 2 minutes. Don't let them color.

2. Remove the pan from the heat and add the eggs, stirring constantly with a spatula so that they scramble lightly. The trick here is to not move them around aggressively, but to use the spatula to pull the mixture gently around the pan—almost like you're cooking an omelet.

3. Return the pan to the heat to finish cooking, gently folding the tomatoes into the eggs.

4. When the eggs are scrambled to your liking, season them well with salt, pepper, and a good squeeze of lime juice. Garnish with cilantro and serve with the toasted pita bread for the best breakfast eggs!

This photo taken
in the Solomon
Islands always
reminds me of
The Life of Pi.

Soups

blackened tomato soup

{ Serves 4 }

Blackening the skin of tomatoes works exceptionally well as a way to make the ingredient taste smoky and interesting. The charring process is what gives this soup its depth.

    This recipe can also be adapted as an excellent chunky chile-tomato sauce that's superb on grilled meat or a burger. You can even bottle it and keep it in the fridge.

5 large tomatoes, quartered (preferably vine ripened—the deeper red, the better!)

¼ red onion

Extra virgin olive oil

Maldon or other flaky salt

Freshly ground black pepper

1 large garlic clove, sliced

1 teaspoon tomato paste

1 tablespoon agave nectar

3 drops Worcestershire sauce (see Notes)

1 to 2 pinches red chile flakes

Plain Greek yogurt, for topping

Fresh cilantro leaves, for garnish

1. Preheat the broiler.

2. Place the tomatoes and onion in a shallow baking dish. Add a couple of lugs of olive oil, season with salt and pepper, and give it a toss. Arrange the tomatoes skin side up so that the broiler blackens and chars the skin.

3. Broil the tomatoes and onion for 15 to 20 minutes, depending on your oven. Check the tomatoes after about 10 minutes and turn the dish if you feel one side is getting more color.

4. When the skin on the tomatoes is black and charred (as in the picture), transfer the contents of the dish to a medium saucepan, making sure you don't lose any of that lovely juice or sticky stuff at the bottom. Get it *all* into the saucepan—this is where so much of your flavor will come from. It's like a beautiful tomato stock/oil.

5. Add the garlic, tomato paste, and just enough water to cover and bring to a simmer over medium heat. Cook for 15 to 20 minutes, until the tomatoes are broken up and soft. Use an immersion blender (easiest—I call this a stab blender) or a freestanding blender to blend the soup. I like it to have a little texture, so I don't blend it all the way, but you may prefer it completely smooth.

6. Pour the soup back into the saucepan and add the agave nectar, Worcestershire sauce, and 1 or 2 pinches of chile flakes, depending on how much heat you'd like.

7. Serve the soup with a dollop of Greek yogurt and some fresh cilantro leaves.

NOTES: *This soup is packed full of vitamins A and C. It's great for your eyes and is loaded with antioxidants. If you want to use this as a sauce instead of a soup, simply omit the water and blend straightaway, without simmering.*

Worcestershire is a strong sauce that's really great for giving depth to dishes like a Bolognese, but make sure you don't add too much. It's intense!

clam soup

{ Serves 3 to 4 }

A lovely winter soup. This base recipe can be served as is, or made into a seafood stew by adding some more vegetables and more shellfish, such as shrimp or mussels. It's great served family-style in the middle of the table with some lovely crusty bread.

Extra virgin olive oil

2 strips of bacon, diced, optional

½ cup thinly sliced leek (white and green parts)

¼ cup finely diced celery

2 garlic cloves, minced, plus 1 smashed garlic clove

⅓ cup sauvignon blanc or other dry white wine

One 6.5-ounce can good-quality clams

¼ red jalapeño chile, seeded and chopped

2 medium carrots, grated (about 1 cup)

1 cup finely diced russet potato

1 teaspoon tomato paste

1 bay leaf

1 pound live clams

Maldon or other flaky salt

Freshly ground black pepper

½ lemon

1 handful fresh flat-leaf parsley leaves, roughly chopped

1. Heat a small lug of olive oil in a medium saucepan over high heat. If you're using bacon, add it now. Cook for 2 to 3 minutes, until the bacon has a little bit of color.

2. Reduce the heat to low and let the pan cool for a minute or two, then add the leek, celery, and garlic and sweat for about 5 minutes, until the leek is translucent. Add the wine and turn the heat up a bit to allow the liquid to reduce.

3. When the liquid has reduced by about one-third, add the clams, including their juice, plus the chile, carrots, potato, tomato paste, bay leaf, and 2 cups of water. Simmer the soup gently for about 30 minutes, until it's at your preferred consistency, giving it a stir every now and then.

4. In the meantime, prepare the live clams by rinsing them under running cold water in a colander. Place them in a steamer, or use the steaming method from the couscous recipe on page 255. Lightly steam for about 10 minutes. You'll know as soon as they're done because their shells will pop open. Don't overcook them, or—as my mom would say—they'll be as leathery as a pair of old boots. Set the finished clams aside.

5. Check the seasoning of the soup; it will want some salt, a good dose of pepper, and a squeeze of lemon juice.

6. To serve, ladle the soup into bowls and top with the steamed clams and parsley.

chilled cucumber, tomato, and sumac soup

{ Serves 4 to 5 }

This is my version of a classic gazpacho. It's bold, confident, and refreshing. Sumac is a wonderful spice used a lot in Middle Eastern cooking. It has a beautiful tart, lemony flavor—if you can't find any, you could substitute the zest of a quarter of a lemon.

½ cucumber, roughly chopped

3 Roma tomatoes, roughly chopped

½ red bell pepper, seeded and roughly chopped

1 teaspoon tomato paste

1 tablespoon red wine vinegar

1 teaspoon ground sumac

1 teaspoon ground cumin

Agave nectar

Maldon or other flaky salt

Freshly ground black pepper

Chopped salad, such as North African Salad (page 91), for serving, optional

1. Put the cucumber, tomatoes, red pepper, tomato paste, vinegar, sumac, cumin, and agave nectar to taste in a blender. Blend until smooth and season with salt and pepper.

2. Refrigerate the soup until it's very, very cold, at least 2 hours.

3. Serve the soup in chilled bowls, topped with a bit of chopped salad if you like. The North African salad works really well here because the flavors are equally punchy in both.

lentil soup

{ Serves 3 }

There are lots of variations on lentil soup out there. This is DVF's favorite. It's incredibly healthy, hearty, and tasty. The mushrooms add a good depth of flavor, and the fresh lemon finishes the soup off well.

Extra virgin olive oil

¼ red onion, finely chopped

½ serrano chile, seeded and chopped

1 large garlic clove, minced or finely grated

¼ cup finely chopped carrot

¼ cup finely chopped celery

1 cup finely chopped button mushrooms

1 heaping teaspoon ground cumin

1 heaping teaspoon ground coriander

1 medium tomato, chopped

¾ cup French green lentils, such as Puy, washed and picked over

4 cups water or vegetable broth

Maldon or other flaky salt

Agave nectar

Freshly ground black pepper

Juice of 1 lemon

Fresh cilantro leaves, optional

1. Heat a good lug of olive oil in a large saucepan over medium-low heat. Add the onion, chile, garlic, carrot, celery, and mushrooms, and sweat for about 5 minutes.

2. Add the cumin and coriander and stir for a couple of minutes. Turn the heat up slightly, so that the spices toast and release their flavor. Add the tomato and cook for another couple of minutes.

3. Add the lentils along with 4 cups of water and a pinch of salt. Bring to a simmer and cook for about 40 minutes. You'll probably have to add more water once or twice, and that's OK, but be careful not to put in

too much liquid—just enough so that nothing sticks to the bottom of the pot. You can always add liquid at the end, but you can't really take it away.

4. After 40 minutes the lentils should be very tender. Pour half of the mixture into a blender and pulse until it's nearly smooth, then add it back into the saucepan with the whole lentils. This gives it a lovely full texture. This step is really up to you and how you prefer the texture of the soup. You may want to blend all of it until very smooth or not blend it at all. Whatever makes you happy.

5. To finish the soup off, add a squeeze of agave nectar. Season with salt and pepper and add the lemon juice. Snip a small handful of fresh cilantro leaves over the top, or serve as is.

sunchoke and cauliflower soup

{ Serves 4 }

The amazing thing about cauliflower is how creamy it is when it's pureed. It's luxurious, smooth, and rich. Also known as Jerusalem artichokes, sunchokes add an interesting flavor to this soup, and are well worth seeking out.

1 tablespoon extra virgin olive oil, plus more for drizzling

¼ red onion, chopped

2 garlic cloves, minced

1 pound sunchokes, peeled and cut into ½-inch pieces (use straightaway or place them in some lemon water until you use them, or else they'll go brown)

¼ cauliflower, cut into chunks, stems included

Vegetable broth

Juice of 1 lemon

Agave nectar

Maldon or other flaky salt

Freshly ground black pepper

1. Heat the olive oil in a medium saucepan over low heat. Add the onion and garlic and sweat for 4 to 5 minutes, until they become slightly translucent, taking care not to let them burn. (*Sweating* is a bit of a chef's term—but a good one to know—for cooking something over low heat in some fat. As a result, the onion and garlic will become beautifully mellow and sweet without any browning.)

2. Add the sunchokes and cauliflower and stir around for a few seconds to infuse the flavors of the onion and garlic oil into the vegetables and make them more intense. Then add just enough vegetable

broth to cover. Bring to a simmer and cook for 15 minutes, or until the cauliflower and sunchokes are fork tender.

3. Using a slotted spoon, transfer the cauliflower and sunchokes to a blender and add a bit of the liquid from the pot. Blend until completely smooth. Then, depending on what consistency you prefer, add more of the cooking liquid from the pot. This soup is meant to be thick and comforting, so be sparing with the liquid. See how you go.

4. Return the soup to the pan to reheat and season with the lemon juice, a touch of agave, salt, and pepper. Pour the soup into bowls and add a drizzle of olive oil to finish it off.

velvety mushroom soup

{ Serves 4 to 6 }

If you love mushrooms, you'll really love this soup. It's incredibly simple and low maintenance—it's really about getting the most out of the mushrooms and letting them shine. Finishing off any mushroom dish with lemon is sure to be a winner, and the garnish of parsley is a clean, fresh addition.

Oh, and just a tip: Be sure to always hold the lid when you're blending soup . . .

2 pounds mixed mushrooms, halved (I use half shiitake and half button)

Maldon or other flaky salt

Freshly ground black pepper

Leaves from 8 fresh thyme sprigs

½ cup extra virgin olive oil, plus more as needed

½ red onion, chopped

1 large garlic clove

Vegetable stock or water

Juice of 1 lemon

⅓ cup Greek feta cheese, optional

1 small handful fresh flat-leaf parsley leaves

1. Preheat the broiler.

2. In a medium bowl, toss the mushrooms with some salt and pepper, the thyme leaves, and olive oil. Spread the mushrooms on a baking sheet in a single layer and place under the broiler. Broil for about 15 minutes, depending on your oven—don't let them burn, but look for a nice brown color to bring out a more intense flavor.

3. Put the browned mushrooms in a medium saucepan over low heat. Important: Reserve any juice or oil from the baking sheet; it's where a lot of the soup's flavor will come from. Add the onion and garlic to the saucepan and cook, stirring, for 5 minutes, or until the onion and garlic have become translucent and soft. If you feel it's too dry, you can add a touch more olive oil.

4. Add the reserved juices from the sheet (even if it doesn't seem like much) and just enough vegetable stock or water to cover the mushrooms. Bring to a boil, then reduce the heat and simmer for 20 minutes, or until the mushrooms are very soft. This stage is all about developing flavors and intensifying them; simmering will make everything more intensely mushroom flavored.

5. Time to blend the soup: Transfer to a blender and blend until very smooth. When you think it's smooth enough, blend even more to take it one step further. This will bring it all the way to velvety.

6. Pour the soup back in the saucepan and check the seasoning. It'll probably need a bit more salt and pepper. Add the lemon juice and give it a little taste again.

7. Pour the hot soup into bowls and garnish it with the feta, if using, and the parsley.

spinach, broccoli, and mint soup

{ Serves 4 }

Just looking at this soup will make you feel healthier—the color is brilliant. I like the idea of not fully cooking the leaves, so that you get all the goodness out of them. Apart from boiling the water, this soup takes about 10 minutes to make. It's the perfect example of how wonderful food can be when you keep it simple.

2 broccoli heads, cut into florets

1 garlic clove

2 handfuls of baby spinach leaves

1 small handful mint

1 small handful basil

Maldon or other flaky salt

Freshly ground black pepper

½ lemon

Agave nectar

1. Bring a pot of water to a boil. Add the broccoli and cook for about 5 minutes, or until the broccoli is tender but still bright green.

2. Remove the pan from the heat. Use a slotted spoon to transfer the broccoli to a blender. Add 2 cups of the cooking water, reserving the rest.

3. Blend until you start to get a smooth puree, then add the spinach and herbs. (If you feel you need to add a bit more water to get it going, go ahead, but I usually leave adding more water until the end when I have a totally smooth mixture. This blending step, as simple as it is, is really important. It's going to feel like a long time, but give it at least 4 to 5 minutes to blend. The soup has the potential to become velvety smooth, so even when you feel like you might have blended it

enough, blend it for another minute. A beautifully smooth texture will make all the difference.)

4. Transfer the mixture to a clean pot and add enough cooking water to reach your desired consistency. Add salt and pepper to taste, the juice of half a lemon, and a squeeze of agave. Taste and adjust the seasoning as necessary. (I like to serve it as is, because it's such a pure soup.)

Food market, West Papua New Guinea.

Opposite page: Food shopping, Papua New Guinea.

Salads

asian slaw with wasabi

{ Serves 3 }

This is a very simple slaw that is ideal served with Beer Tempura (page 229) or as an accompaniment to a piece of grilled fish or seafood.

2 tablespoons minced red onion

6 scallions, thinly sliced

½ red cabbage, cored and thinly sliced

Juice of 1 lime

¼ cup mayonnaise

½ to 1 tablespoon prepared wasabi (depending on how spicy you like it)

1 small garlic clove, minced

Small squeeze of agave nectar

2 tablespoons rice vinegar

Maldon salt or other flaky salt

Freshly ground black pepper

1 handful fresh cilantro leaves, roughly chopped

A few fresh basil leaves, roughly chopped

1. In a large bowl, combine the red onion, scallions, and cabbage. Set aside.

2. In a separate bowl, make the dressing by combining the lime juice, mayonnaise, wasabi, garlic, agave nectar, and vinegar. Season with salt and pepper.

3. When you're ready to serve, toss the cabbage mixture in the dressing, add the cilantro and basil, and toss to coat. Transfer to a clean bowl and serve.

NOTE: *If you want to make this in advance, keep the dressing and salad separate until you are ready to serve. It's best eaten straightaway but will keep in the fridge for a day or two.*

brie, grape, and arugula salad

{ Serves 2 }

A good friend of mine, Becky, worked with me on *Eos*, and we circumnavigated the world together. If I ever asked her what salad she wanted, it didn't matter what country we happened to be in—this is the one she chose. It's vibrant, fresh, and fragrant and topped with beautifully creamy Brie. So here you go, Becky—this is your salad. Enjoy.

dressing

1 tablespoon balsamic vinegar

Squeeze of agave nectar

Extra virgin olive oil

Maldon or other flaky salt

Freshly ground black pepper

salad

½ cup pine nuts

Large handful baby arugula

Leaves from 3 fresh tarragon sprigs

Leaves from 3 fresh dill sprigs

1½ cups seedless grapes, quartered

4 to 5 ounces good-quality Brie cheese, chilled

1. To make the dressing, whisk the vinegar, agave nectar, olive oil, and salt and pepper to taste in a bowl. Adjust the seasoning as desired, and set aside.

2. To make the salad, toast the pine nuts in a small dry skillet over low heat for 3 to 4 minutes, until evenly browned. Remove from the heat and set aside.

3. Toss the arugula, tarragon, dill, grapes, and pine nuts in a bowl.

4. Cut the Brie into bite-size pieces. (Make sure the cheese is nice and cold; that way it won't stick to your knife or melt.)

5. When you're ready to serve, toss the salad with the dressing and top with the Brie.

NOTE: *Avoid buying aged Brie for this salad—it won't hold as well, and it will be a little too strong for this fresh salad.*

bright green pea salad
with lemon and mint

{ Serves 4 to 6 }

This salad is like a pea family reunion. It's very simple, but the goat cheese makes it a bit more substantial and luxurious. The inspiration for this recipe was a request for a bright, all-green salad. You can stick with using peas, or add whatever other green vegetables you find at the market.

¼ pound haricots verts, ends trimmed (green beans are fine if you can't find haricots verts)

¼ pound snap peas, halved

¼ pound snow peas, halved

¼ pound fresh peas, shelled

¼ pound fava beans, shelled and peeled

1 celery stalk, thinly sliced on the diagonal

Juice of 1 Meyer lemon

Extra virgin olive oil

Maldon or other flaky salt

Freshly ground black pepper

1 handful yellow pea shoots, optional

1 handful green pea shoots, optional

1 handful fresh mint leaves, roughly torn, optional

¼ pound good-quality goat cheese, optional

1. Bring a large saucepan of water to a boil over medium-high heat and prepare a large bowl of ice water.

2. Throw the haricots verts (which take the longest to cook) into the pot of boiling water. After 30 seconds, add the snap peas and snow peas. Add the fresh peas and fava beans after another 30 seconds—these will cook fastest. (Adding the beans in intervals of 30 seconds will save you the time of boiling multiple pots of water and cooking each vegetable individually.)

3. When the beans turn bright green and tender but are still very crisp, transfer the peas and beans to the ice water to stop the cooking. When they are cold, drain and transfer to a large glass bowl; add the celery.

4. Just when you're ready to serve the salad, add the lemon juice, some olive oil, and salt and pepper to taste and give the salad a good toss with your hands. Mix in the pea shoots and mint, if using. If using the goat cheese, gently crumble it in with your hands. Transfer to a serving bowl and serve.

NOTE: *Don't be tempted to dress the salad too far in advance. The lemon can discolor the greens and ruin the aesthetic of the dish, which, in my opinion, is half the pleasure of it.*

celeriac, green apple, and fennel salad

{ Serves 4 to 6 }

This is a classic combination of ingredients, and for a good reason: The flavors of celeriac, apple, and fennel work so well together. DVF loves the crunch and freshness of raw vegetables, so I try to slip them in a salad whenever I can.

I don't have a problem with consuming raw egg yolk, but I know many people aren't comfortable with it. This recipe involves pasteurizing the eggs, which ensures their safety. And it's a lot less hassle than it sounds.

dressing	salad
1 egg yolk	1½ green apples
Juice of ½ lemon	1 medium celeriac, peeled
1 teaspoon fresh thyme leaves	1 fennel root, halved and outer layer removed
1 teaspoon agave nectar	⅓ cup sliced almonds
1 teaspoon Dijon mustard	1 handful fresh parsley leaves
2 tablespoons extra virgin olive oil	1 small handful fresh dill, roughly chopped
Maldon or other flaky salt	
Freshly ground black pepper	

1. To make the dressing, combine the egg yolk and lemon juice in a metal bowl over a saucepan of simmering water and whisk for about 30 seconds. Make sure the bowl doesn't get too hot, or the egg will start to scramble. As soon as bubbles start to form, take it off the heat. Keep whisking, and the egg will thicken. Add the thyme, agave nectar, mustard, olive oil, and salt and pepper to taste. When the dressing

starts getting a little thicker, add a bit of water. Check the seasoning and set aside.

2. Using a mandoline, cut the apples, celeriac, and fennel into wafer-thin slices. Set aside.

3. In a small dry skillet over low heat, toast the almonds for 3 to 4 minutes, until evenly browned, stirring or tossing often and taking care that they don't burn.

4. In a salad bowl, toss the apples, celeriac, and fennel with the almonds, parsley, and dill. Add the dressing and gently toss the salad.

NOTE: *If you're entertaining, this salad should not be prepared too far in advance, or it will wilt and discolor.*

mexican bean and citrus salad

{ Serves 4 to 6 }

This is a super-quick and easy summer salad to go alongside any Mexican meal or barbecue. You can make heaps of it at a time, and it actually gets better after a few days in the fridge because the beans soak up the flavor. If you do save it for a few days, check the seasoning again and freshen it up with some more fresh cilantro and a squeeze of lime before you serve.

I like to make this for the guys I work with—they spend hours lifting weights in the gym and then look for ways to put as much protein into their bodies as they can, so this salad does the trick.

One 15-ounce can pinto beans (or any other beans you like)

One 15-ounce can black beans

One 15-ounce can cannellini beans

6 scallions, trimmed, white and light green parts sliced on the diagonal

2 tablespoons chopped fresh oregano

1 large handful fresh cilantro leaves, roughly chopped

Zest of 1 orange

Juice of ½ orange

Juice of 1½ limes

1 tablespoon extra virgin olive oil

Maldon or other flaky salt

Freshly ground black pepper

Drain the beans in a colander and rinse them under cold water. Shake off the excess water. In a large bowl, combine the beans, scallions, oregano, cilantro, orange zest, and orange and lime juices. Toss with the olive oil and season with salt and pepper. Give it a good mix and check the seasoning. If you want more zing, add a bit more lime, and if you want more sweetness, add more orange juice. The salad works really well when there's a nice balance between the two.

endive, pomegranate, and manchego salad with yogurt dressing

{ Serves 2 }

This is a lovely, delicate salad. Try to get both the white and purple endives to make it even more colorful and pretty.

NOTE: *If you're making this salad in advance, prep the endive leaves, wrap them in wet paper towels, and place them in the fridge. Keep all the ingredients separate until you're ready to plate.*

yogurt dressing

2 tablespoons plain yogurt

1 teaspoon fresh lemon juice

1 teaspoon agave nectar

¼ garlic clove, minced

Maldon or other flaky salt

Freshly ground black pepper

salad

3 Belgian endives, a mix of white and purple if possible, roots trimmed

½ cup shaved Manchego cheese (use a vegetable peeler)

½ cup pomegranate seeds

¼ cup fresh dill leaves

1. To make the dressing, whisk the yogurt, lemon juice, agave nectar, garlic, and salt and pepper to taste in a bowl. Carefully add a few drops of water, and whisk again until the dressing is just pourable but still holds together. Check the seasoning and add more lemon, agave, or salt if necessary.

2. To make the salad, separate the leaves of the endives and arrange on a large plate or platter. Top with the Manchego, pomegranate seeds, and dill.

3. Just before serving, drizzle the dressing over the salad.

grapefruit, watercress, and carrot salad

{ Serves 3 to 4 }

This salad is happiness in a bowl! Eating it instantly makes me feel alive and well. The juicy grapefruit, crisp carrots, and peppery watercress matched with the bold cilantro and creamy pistachio is exciting eating.

⅓ cup shelled pistachios

2 grapefruits, segmented (see photos, below and page 84)

1 large handful watercress

2 carrots, shaved on a mandoline and placed in ice water (see photo, page 84)

1 handful fresh cilantro leaves, picked and roughly torn or chopped

dressing

2 tablespoons grapefruit juice (after removing the segments, squeeze what's left of the grapefruit body to get this juice—there probably will be enough for a small glass of juice for you too)

1 tablespoon extra virgin olive oil

Small squeeze of agave nectar

Pinch Maldon or other flaky salt

Freshly ground black pepper to taste

1. In a small dry skillet over medium-low heat, toast the pistachios until evenly browned, 3 to 4 minutes, stirring frequently. Remove from the heat and set aside.

2. Combine the grapefruits, watercress, carrots, and cilantro in a bowl and use your hands to toss gently.

3. Whisk the dressing ingredients in a small bowl. When you're ready to serve, add the nuts and dressing to the salad.

NOTE: *It's important to leave the nuts out until the last minute so that they stay nice and crunchy.*

green bean, tomato, and potato salad

{ Serves 4 }

Potato salad usually makes me think of heavy egg-and-mayonnaise mixtures, but this recipe is nothing like that. It's just a great green bean salad with a lot of flavor—and potatoes. I've used Kewpie mayonnaise in this recipe, which is a favorite. It's a Japanese version of mayonnaise that is creamier and smoother than the American classic and can be found at specialty stores.

Maldon or other flaky salt

1 pound mixed small potatoes (thin-skinned new potatoes are great here)

5 ounces green beans, ends trimmed, halved

1 garlic clove, minced

2 tablespoons finely chopped red onion

2 whole scallions, thinly sliced

1 cup cherry tomatoes, halved

2 tablespoons extra virgin olive oil

2 tablespoons mayonnaise, preferably Kewpie

2 tablespoons sherry vinegar

1 teaspoon agave nectar

⅓ cup roughly chopped fresh dill

⅓ cup roughly chopped fresh parsley

1. Bring a saucepan of salted water to a boil and add the potatoes. Cook until fork-tender, about 8 minutes; drain. Break up the potatoes a little bit, but don't mash them.

2. Bring a saucepan of salted water to a boil again and add the green beans. Cook for just under

a minute, taking care not to overcook them. Drain the green beans under cold running water to stop the cooking.

3. Meanwhile, in a large glass bowl, combine the garlic, onion, scallions, tomatoes, olive oil, mayonnaise, vinegar, and agave nectar. Add the potatoes while they're still very hot so they can soak up the dressing. Mix in the green beans, then set aside to let cool to room temperature.

4. Stir in the dill and parsley and check the seasoning just before serving.

NOTE: *If you're storing this for later use, place the bowl in the fridge and add the herbs just before serving.*

marinated cucumber and chile salad

{ Serves 2 to 3 }

This is a great salad to pair with Chickpea and Corn Falafel (page 235). I first learned about using habañero chiles to marinate cucumber from a cashier at Whole Foods, and he was so right. My mouth is watering thinking about it.

A couple things about habañeros: The chile won't stay as hot when it's refrigerated, so don't be scared to use as much as or more than the recipe calls for. Just be sure to wash your board and your hands well after you've prepared the chile. And whatever you do, don't fiddle with your contact lenses or touch your eyes anytime soon. I made that mistake a few years ago. Ouch.

1 cucumber, seeded, quartered lengthwise, and sliced on the diagonal

½ habañero chile, seeded and finely chopped

¼ cup finely chopped red onion

1 tablespoon extra virgin olive oil

Squeeze of agave nectar

Juice of 1 lemon

Maldon or other flaky salt

Freshly ground black pepper

1. Place the cucumber, chile, and onion in a glass bowl. Toss with the olive oil, agave nectar, and lemon juice; season with salt and pepper.

2. Set in the fridge for at least an hour before eating or up to a day.

marinated tomato and chile salad with buffalo mozzarella

{ Serves 4 to 6 }

I really love that this salad produces so much flavor with so little effort. One of the best parts is the juice that's left over on the plate. When I make this for DVF, she patiently waits for her guests to serve themselves, and then she'll pour the beautiful tomato dressing over her whole plate of food.

dressing

½ serrano chile, thinly sliced (I keep the seeds in for a kick, but check yours—it might be too much)

1 garlic clove, minced

Leaves from 2 fresh oregano sprigs

2 tablespoons red wine vinegar

1 tablespoon agave nectar

⅓ cup extra virgin olive oil

Maldon or other flaky salt

Freshly ground black pepper

salad

6 large assorted tomatoes (the more colors and varieties, the better—deep red, green, yellow, Roma, beefsteak, heirloom)

1 cup cherry tomatoes—again, mixed colors would be ideal

About 10 ounces fresh buffalo mozzarella

About 8 fresh basil leaves

1 handful fresh flat-leaf parsley

1. To make the dressing, whisk together the chile, garlic, oregano, vinegar, agave nectar, olive oil, salt and pepper to taste in a bowl. Set aside for at least 10 minutes to infuse.

2. To make the salad, cut the large tomatoes into fairly thin slices and place them haphazardly on a serving platter. Halve or quarter the cherry tomatoes and sprinkle them on top of the tomatoes.

3. Lay the mozzarella on paper towels to drain the excess liquid. Tear the cheese into bite-size pieces and place them on top of the tomatoes.

4. Give the chile dressing another quick mix and taste it for seasoning. If it's good to go, get a large spoon and slowly drizzle it over the salad, making sure that every part of the salad is covered with dressing.

5. Let the salad sit for at least 5 minutes before serving to give the tomatoes a little time to suck in some of that wonderful dressing, or cover and refrigerate if you're not serving it immediately.

6. When you're about to serve, tear the basil over the top and scatter with the parsley.

north african salad

{ Serves 4 }

Sumac is one of my favorite spices. It's zingy and fresh, and it's really what makes this salad special. It's definitely worth going to the effort to get, and it's becoming more readily available in supermarkets—it's lovely in other salad dressings or simply sprinkled on fresh tomatoes, so you'll definitely find other uses for it.

This salad is incredibly tasty, simple, and summery.

Extra virgin olive oil

1 large pita bread, cut into ½-inch cubes

Maldon or other flaky salt

Freshly ground black pepper

½ English cucumber, seeded and diced

3 tomatoes, seeded and diced

½ red onion, finely chopped

1 scallion, thinly sliced

½ garlic clove, minced

1 radish, thinly sliced

½ red bell pepper, seeded and diced

1 cup loosely packed fresh flat-leaf
  parsley leaves

½ cup loosely packed fresh mint leaves

½ cup loosely packed fresh dill leaves
  (no big stems)

Juice of ½ lemon

1 teaspoon ground sumac

Agave nectar

1. In a skillet, heat 1 tablespoon olive oil, add the pita cubes, and toast until golden. Season with salt and pepper and set aside to cool.

2. In a glass bowl, mix the cucumber, tomatoes, onion, scallion, garlic, radish, bell pepper, and herbs. Toss with the lemon juice, sumac, and 1 tablespoon of olive oil. Add a little squeeze of agave nectar just to even out the lemony punch of the sumac. Check the seasoning and adjust to your taste.

3. Mix in the pita croutons when you're ready to serve so they stay lovely and crispy.

middle eastern watermelon salad

{ Serves 2 }

This salad is so vibrant and inviting when it's plated. You won't expect the orange citrus flavor, but it works so well with the watermelon. With the extra bite and crunch of salty feta and toasted sesame seeds, this is a salad you'll keep going back to.

2 tablespoons sesame seeds

¼ watermelon, cut into large dice

½ cup crumbled feta cheese

Heaping 1 cup pomegranate seeds, optional

1 small handful fresh mint leaves, torn

1 small handful fresh cilantro leaves, torn

½ orange

Extra virgin olive oil

Freshly ground black pepper

1. In a small skillet, toast the sesame seeds over low heat, stirring frequently, about 3 minutes. Remove from the heat and set aside.

2. Arrange the watermelon and feta on a flat plate. Sprinkle the pomegranate seeds, sesame seeds, mint, and cilantro over the top.

3. When you're ready to serve, squeeze the juice of the orange over the salad and drizzle it with olive oil. Finish with some cracked black pepper and serve.

panzanella salad

{ Serves 4 }

Italy brings back so many happy food memories for me. The first time I ever had this salad was in Genoa, and I couldn't get over what a great idea it was to put bread in a salad—it soaks up all the goodness of the tomatoes and dressing; all the leftover juices you'd want to mop up after the salad is finished are already taken care of for you. This is the quintessential Italian summer salad. You could serve it with a simple grilled piece of beef to make a really fantastic meal.

½ loaf stale bread (sourdough or baguette is best)

4 large beefsteak tomatoes

1 tablespoon roughly chopped fresh oregano

1 garlic clove, minced

¼ red onion, thinly sliced

1½ tablespoons red wine vinegar

Agave nectar

Maldon or other flaky salt

Freshly ground black pepper

¼ cup extra virgin olive oil

1 small handful Kalamata olives

8 ounces fresh mozzarella cheese

8 large fresh basil leaves

1 small handful fresh flat-leaf parsley leaves

1. To prep the bread, remove any hard, thick crust and cut it into 1½-inch cubes. Set aside.

2. Cut the tomatoes into quarters and remove the seeds from the flesh of the tomatoes. Place the seeds and a good pinch of salt into a sieve resting over a bowl. (This will help them to release their wonderful juices, which you'll add to the dressing in step 5.) Let the seeds sit for at least 15 minutes.

3. Cut the tomatoes in half again, place them in a medium bowl, and set aside.

4. To make the dressing, combine the oregano, garlic, and onion in a small bowl and add the vinegar; season with agave nectar, salt, and pepper to taste. Whisk in the olive oil.

5. After at least 15 minutes, use your hands to gently squeeze the tomato seeds over the sieve so that they release their juice into the bowl. Add this juice to the dressing and taste for seasoning. Pour the dressing over the bread and toss. Let sit for at least another 5 to 10 minutes.

6. Add the tomatoes and olives and give the salad a gentle toss with your hands. Add the mozzarella by tearing it gently into the salad.

7. Garnish with torn basil leaves and parsley and serve.

rice noodle, avocado, and beef salad

{ Serves 4 to 6 }

When I traveled on *Eos* to Vietnam, I ate many variations of this type of salad. The Vietnamese are incredibly good at making simple but vibrant food, with some intense flavors.

2½ pounds strip steak or rib eye steak (about 2 steaks)

Maldon or other flaky salt

Freshly ground black pepper

Canola or vegetable oil

3½ ounces thin rice noodles

2 avocados (slightly firm is perfect)

Juice of 1 lime

marinade

¼ cup soy sauce

½ teaspoon fish sauce

2 teaspoons sugar

Juice of 1 lime

dressing

1 tablespoon minced ginger

Juice of 1 lime

5 tablespoons rice wine vinegar

1 teaspoon fish sauce

1½ teaspoons sugar

¼ cup finely chopped fresh cilantro

1 small handful fresh mint leaves

1 small handful fresh cilantro leaves

1 small handful fresh basil leaves

1 small handful cashews, lightly toasted and crushed

1. Place a sauté pan over high heat and get the pan really hot. Season the steaks well with salt and pepper and rub a little oil on both sides. Place them in the smoking hot pan and cook for 3 to 4 minutes on each side, depending on how well you want your meat to be cooked.

I think medium rare to medium is good for this dish. Place the steaks on a plate, pour any pan juices on top, and set aside to rest.

2. Bring a saucepan of water to a boil and add the rice noodles. Cook for about 3 minutes, or according to the package directions. Be careful not to overcook them—these noodles are really thin.

3. Make a quick marinade by combining the marinade ingredients in a medium bowl.

4. Drain the noodles in a colander and run them under cold water to stop the cooking. Give the colander a shake to remove the excess water and place the noodles in the bowl with the marinade. Give it a good toss to coat the noodles well and set aside.

5. Prep the avocados by peeling, removing the pit, and cutting them into slices; toss with the lime juice and set aside.

6. Combine all the dressing ingredients in a small bowl. (It'll taste quite sharp but will be great over the salad.)

7. To assemble the salad: Give the noodles a final toss in the marinade and place them on a platter, pulling them apart a bit. Cut the steaks into ½-inch slices and drape the strips of beef over the noodles, then tuck them in, around, and under the noodles. Do the same with the avocado slices. Finally, use a spoon to dress the salad, distributing the dressing as evenly as possible. Roughly tear the mint, cilantro, and basil leaves and scatter them over the salad, along with the toasted cashews. Serve immediately.

simple avocado, arugula, and spinach salad

{ Serves 2 }

This is a simple salad that can be served alongside lots of different dishes—grilled fish or a piece of grilled beef—or just eaten by itself. And it's as easy as it is simple.

Avocado adds a wonderful richness to any salad, and leaving it to stand with the lemon juice and other ingredients makes it slightly creamy.

1 handful cherry tomatoes, halved

1 avocado, cut into bite-size pieces

1 tablespoon finely chopped red onion

About 5 Kalamata olives, pitted and halved

Maldon or other flaky salt

Freshly ground black pepper

Extra virgin olive oil

1 squeeze agave nectar

Juice of ½ lemon

1 large handful baby spinach leaves

1 large handful baby arugula leaves

Leaves from 1 fresh dill sprig, roughly chopped

1. In a bowl, combine the tomatoes, avocado, red onion, and olives. Add a pinch of salt, a good twist of black pepper, a lug of olive oil, the agave nectar, and the lemon juice.

2. Stir to mix everything up and let stand for at least 5 minutes or up to a few hours. When you're ready to eat, mix in the spinach, arugula, and dill.

tomato and egg salad

{ Serves 4 }

This is my version of a South African–style salad. It feels like what I would have at someone's house with a barbecue. In fact, I probably have had it at a barbecue in South Africa. If I stole the idea of this recipe from someone, I'm sorry, but thank you—it's delicious.

3 organic, free-range eggs

3 tomatoes, cut into wedges

2 tablespoons finely chopped red onion

2 tablespoons white vinegar

1½ tablespoons extra virgin olive oil

Maldon or other flaky salt

Freshly ground black pepper

1 handful fresh cilantro leaves, roughly chopped

1. Place the eggs in a saucepan full of cold water (this keeps the eggs from cracking) and bring to a boil over high heat. When the water reaches a boil, cook for just under 6 minutes.

2. In a glass bowl, combine the tomatoes, red onion, vinegar, and olive oil. Give it a toss and season with salt and pepper. (Get most of your tossing done before adding the eggs to keep them from falling apart.)

3. When the eggs are cooked, peel them and cut into quarters. Add the eggs to the bowl and check the seasoning. Add the cilantro and give it another gentle toss.

spinach, pomegranate, dill, and cilantro chopped salad

{ Serves 2 }

This is prepared the same way as the Chopped Arugula and Basil Salad that accompanies Beef Tagliata (page 181). It's super-easy but also delicious. I sometimes serve it with the Chicken and Beef Koftas (page 186) by spreading the salad on a platter, then tucking the little meat bundles in and around the wonderful dressed leaves.

2 handfuls baby spinach leaves	1 tablespoon extra virgin olive oil
1 large handful fresh cilantro leaves	Juice of ½ lemon
1 handful fresh dill leaves	½ cup pomegranate seeds
1 garlic clove	Maldon or other flaky salt
Agave nectar	Freshly ground black pepper

1. Put the spinach, cilantro, dill, and garlic on a cutting board and roughly chop (for a demonstration of the method, see page 189). Transfer to a bowl.

2. Add agave nectar to taste, the olive oil, lemon juice, and pomegranate seeds. Season with salt and pepper. Give it a toss with your hands and serve it on its own.

trout, pear, and mâche salad with hazelnut dressing

{ Serves 4 }

This salad is beautiful and delicate. It has hardly any ingredients, but it's wonderful. The Nut Salad Dressing can really work well with just about any salad.

2 pieces cooked trout (see page 157), chilled

1 unpeeled pear (preferably Bosc)

1 lemon

3 handfuls fresh mâche lettuce

1 small handful fresh dill, chopped (no big stems)

¼ cup hazelnuts, toasted and skinned, optional

Nut Salad Dressing (page 286)

1. Make sure the flesh of the trout is cold, then gently peel the skin back. If it was cooked well (which yours will be), it'll peel off easily. Using a knife, slide the flesh off the bone, away from the spine in the middle of the fillet. Once you get started, it's a pretty easy process. Check the beautiful flakes for bones.

2. Thinly slice the pear and place it in a bowl. Squeeze some lemon juice on top to coat and gently toss.

3. Plate the trout on a platter, not in a bowl. Scatter the pear, mâche, dill, and hazelnuts around the fish. Dress generously with the Nut Salad Dressing and serve.

white bean salad

{ Serves 4 to 6 }

This is another salad that is versatile as an accompaniment or on its own. I like to eat it with some grilled, marinated chicken thighs or tossed with some arugula to make it a complete meal.

Haloumi cheese is one of my favorites. Some people call it squeaky cheese because of the noise it can make in your mouth when you chew it. I love it for that, and its briny flavor.

Two 15-ounce cans cannellini beans, drained and rinsed

¼ red onion, finely chopped

1 garlic clove, minced

1 teaspoon agave nectar

Juice of 1½ lemons

1 zucchini, julienned on a mandoline

Maldon or other flaky salt

Freshly ground black pepper

2 tablespoons Hummus (page 283), or extra virgin olive oil

4 ounces haloumi cheese, cut into ½-inch-long matchsticks

1 handful fresh flat-leaf parsley leaves, roughly chopped

1 large handful fresh cilantro leaves, roughly chopped

1. Combine the beans, onion, garlic, agave nectar, lemon juice, zucchini, salt and pepper in a large bowl and mix until everything is well integrated. If you're going to use Hummus, add it here. I really recommend that you do, as it adds a wonderful richness to the dish, but if you're doing without, add a good lug of olive oil. Let stand at room temperature to marinate for at least 30 minutes or up to an hour.

2. Meanwhile, prepare the haloumi cheese by heating up a skillet and adding the strips of cheese to the dry hot pan. Cook for about 40 seconds on each side, until you get some nice color. Note: If you're not serving immediately, put the grilled strips of cheese on a small baking sheet and place them in the oven for a few minutes to heat up prior to serving.

3. When you're ready to serve, mix the herbs into the salad and give it one last taste for seasoning, then top it with the haloumi cheese.

beet and orange salad with a citrus-cumin vinaigrette

{ Serves 2 to 3 }

A great salad to accompany a tagine-style dish—it's alive with texture and color and the taste is uncomplicated. I try to get blood oranges when I can, to pair with golden beets, but it'll be just as beautiful with purple beets and bright navel oranges. To get the beets into these little strips, I use a Benriner mandoline (see Tools, page 19).

dressing

¼ cup freshly squeezed orange juice

1 tablespoon freshly squeezed lemon juice

2 tablespoons extra virgin olive oil

1 teaspoon ground cumin

Maldon or other flaky salt

Freshly ground black pepper

salad

2 medium beets, peeled and julienned on a mandoline

2 oranges, peeled and sliced

1 handful fresh cilantro leaves

1. Whisk all the dressing ingredients together and check the seasoning.

2. When you're ready to serve, toss the beets, oranges, cilantro, and dressing together.

Streetside
restaurant,
Vietnam.

Opposite page:
Market, Vietnam.

Grains

green apple and macadamia quinoa

{ Serves 4 }

This dish tastes like health and summer. It can be eaten as a side dish or on its own.

1 cup uncooked quinoa

½ cup macadamia nuts

1 small garlic clove, minced

1 small green onion, thinly sliced

¾ cup seeded diced cucumber

1 cup diced green apple

½ cup diced green bell pepper

¼ cup diced celery

½ red serrano chile, seeded and thinly sliced

Juice of 1 lemon

Agave nectar

2 tablespoons plain yogurt

Maldon or other flaky salt

1. Prepare the quinoa according to the package directions. Put the drained quinoa back into the pot and stir it over low heat to remove some of the moisture.

2. In a small dry skillet, toast the macadamia nuts over medium low heat until evenly browned, 3 to 4 minutes, stirring often to keep them from burning. Crush the nuts lightly with a knife.

3. In a large bowl, combine the quinoa, macadamia nuts, and the remaining ingredients. Toss and check for seasoning; add more lemon juice and salt if necessary.

pomegranate, nut, and green herb quinoa

{ Serves 2 }

This is the first quinoa I made for DVF. I remember being nervous about cooking for her, but she loved it—she has a wonderful appreciation for bold, vibrant food.

Pair this with Chicken and Beef Koftas (page 186).

1 cup uncooked quinoa

½ small red onion, finely chopped

1 small garlic clove, minced

1 teaspoon extra virgin olive oil

1½ tablespoons Hummus (page 283)

Maldon or other flaky salt

Freshly ground black pepper

Juice of 1 to 2 lemons

½ cup macadamia nuts, toasted

½ cup sliced almonds, toasted

½ cup hazelnuts, toasted

1½ cups pomegranate seeds

1 handful fresh dill, roughly chopped (no big stems)

1 handful fresh flat-leaf parsley leaves, roughly chopped

1 small handful fresh mint leaves, roughly chopped

1. Prepare the quinoa according to the package directions.

2. While the quinoa is cooking, combine the onion, garlic, olive oil, and Hummus in a large glass bowl.

3. Drain the quinoa and put it back in the pot. Stir it over low heat for a couple of minutes to steam off some of the excess water.

4. Add the quinoa to the glass bowl, season with salt and pepper, and add the lemon juice.

5. Loosely cover the mixture and let it sit until it comes to room temperature. If you are not serving immediately, refrigerate and bring to room temperature before serving.

6. When you're ready to serve, mix the nuts, pomegranate seeds, and herbs with the quinoa and toss with your hands. Check the seasoning. Remember, when food sits for a while, especially in the fridge, the cold tones down the seasoning, so add a bit more lemon, salt, or pepper if you need to.

roast vegetable risoni

{ Serves 4 to 6 }

A really easy, really quick side that's great for a barbecue or picnic. It can be made in advance, which is great too.

1 zucchini, cut into ½-inch-thick diagonal slices

1 medium eggplant, cut into about 1-inch × 2-inch pieces

¼ red onion, roughly chopped into about ½-inch pieces

1 handful brown mushrooms, roughly chopped

3 tomatoes, each cut into 8 wedges

7 fresh thyme sprigs

Maldon or other flaky salt

Freshly ground black pepper

Extra virgin olive oil

2 cups risoni, or orzo (see Note)

2 tablespoons sherry vinegar or balsamic vinegar

4 ounces good-quality feta cheese, crumbled

1 small handful fresh basil leaves, torn into unequal-size pieces

1. Preheat the oven to 500°F and bring a pot of lightly salted water to a boil.

2. On a baking sheet lined with wax paper, combine the zucchini, eggplant, onion, mushrooms, and tomatoes. Pull the thyme leaves off the stems and sprinkle them on the veggies, along with salt, lots of pepper, and about 3 tablespoons of olive oil. Give it a good mix with your hands and roast for about 15 minutes, until the vegetables have softened and roasted with some good color, which will bring out wonderful flavors.

3. Place the risoni in the boiling water and cook until al dente, about 10 minutes. Drain and place in a large bowl with a drizzle of olive oil to prevent sticking.

4. Add the vegetables and any juices that have been released during cooking to the risoni. Add the vinegar and feta and give it a good mix around. Taste to check the seasoning.

5. If you're going to serve it straightaway, sprinkle the fresh basil over the dish and gently toss to distribute. If you're going to serve it later, cover with plastic wrap and refrigerate. Bring to room temperature before serving (it should not be served cold) and add the basil, along with a drizzle of olive oil and salt and pepper to taste.

NOTE: *Risoni (also called orzo) is a form of pasta that looks like rice. I really love its texture. It's super-versatile and a nice change from other pastas. Even just a simple risoni tossed in basil, dill, and parsley with lemon juice and pine nuts is delicious. Give that a try too.*

pearl barley with baby spinach, corn, and shiitake mushrooms

{ Serves 3 to 4 }

Pearl barley is used a lot in stews and soups, but I think it works really well in a salad like this. If you mix it when it's hot, the barley acts like a little sponge and soaks up all the flavors. You can try using barley in place of the quinoa in the Pomegranate, Nut, and Green Herb Quinoa (page 119) too.

¾ cup pearl barley

½ cup pine nuts

¼ red onion, finely chopped

Extra virgin olive oil

3½ ounces shiitake mushrooms, stalks
    removed and caps cut into quarters

1 ear corn

⅓ cup Hummus (page 283)

Maldon or other flaky salt

Freshly ground black pepper

½ lemon

1 handful baby spinach leaves

½ cup fresh dill leaves (no big stems)

½ cup fresh flat-leaf parsley leaves

1. Bring a pot of salted water to a boil. Add the barley and cook for about 30 minutes, until tender.

2. While the barley is cooking, toast the pine nuts in a small dry skillet over low heat until lightly browned, about 3 minutes, stirring often to keep them from burning. Combine the pine nuts and onion in a large bowl.

3. Using the same skillet over high heat, add a tablespoon of olive oil and the mushrooms. Sauté for about 4 minutes, until the mushrooms

have some good color. Add them to the bowl with the onion and pine nuts.

4. Again in the same skillet over medium-high heat, add some more olive oil if necessary and the corncob. Cook the corn for about 5 minutes, until it's nicely colored all over. (It'll make a bit of noise and spit a tiny bit, but don't worry—the heat shouldn't be high enough to make it pop and splatter!) Remove it from the skillet and place it on a cutting board to cool down.

5. Drain the barley and add it to the bowl along with the Hummus, season with salt and pepper. Cut the corn kernels off the cob and add them too. Give it a taste, then squeeze in the juice from the lemon half.

6. Add the baby spinach leaves and mix well. Garnish with the dill and parsley and serve.

quinoa risotto

{ Serves 4 }

I love risotto but rarely eat it because I always feel so heavy and slow afterward. Making it with quinoa instead of rice gives you the wonderful taste and comfort of risotto without all that starch. This is a DVF favorite.

2 to 3 tablespoons extra virgin olive oil

⅓ cup finely chopped red onion

1 or 2 garlic cloves, minced

1 cup uncooked quinoa

1 cup sauvignon blanc or other white wine

Maldon or other flaky sea salt

2 cups water or vegetable broth, plus more as needed

1 cup green beans cut into 1-inch pieces

¼ to ½ cup green peas

½ cup lima beans

1 cup asparagus cut into 1-inch pieces

½ cup shelled fava beans

3 tablespoons crème fraîche

1 cup freshly grated Parmesan cheese

Juice of ½ lemon

Freshly ground black pepper

1 small handful fresh dill leaves, roughly chopped (no big stems)

1 handful fresh flat-leaf parsley, roughly chopped

1 handful fresh mint leaves, roughly chopped

1. Heat the olive oil in a saucepan over low heat. Add the onion and garlic and sweat for about 4 minutes, until softened.

2. Add the quinoa, give it a good stir, and let it toast for about a minute. You'll hear it start to crackle.

3. The next steps are the same ones you'd follow with risotto: Add the liquid in thirds to let the quinoa soak up each batch of liquid before the next addition. First add the wine and a bit of salt and let the liquid

cook out, stirring occasionally, about 4 minutes. When there's almost no more liquid in the pot, add 1 cup of the stock, give it a good stir, and again let that cook out gently for another 5 minutes or so, stirring occasionally, then repeat with the remaining cup of stock. These steps will take about 15 minutes. If at the end of the 3 additions of liquid the quinoa isn't completely cooked, add a bit more stock and cook it out until the quinoa is done to your taste.

4. Add the green beans, peas, lima beans, asparagus, fava beans, and ½ cup water to the pan. If there's no liquid in the pan, add more to allow the ingredients to cook a little more easily and to keep the dish moist. Turn the heat up a little and partially cover the pan to give the vegetables a cook.

5. When the vegetables are cooked and bright green, remove the saucepan from the heat. Add the crème fraîche, Parmesan, and lemon juice and check the seasoning.

6. Just before you're about to serve, throw in all the beautiful herbs and stir well.

pale ale and shiitake pasta

{ Serves 2 }

You know that feeling when you do something, and suddenly it makes so much sense that you wonder: *How did I not do this before?* That's how I felt about this recipe. I was making myself a quick mushroom pasta and would usually add white wine, but I was drinking a beer at the time, so I added that instead. What an amazing combination—shiitake mushrooms and beer! It's really earthy and wonderful and works so well for this easy, tasty pasta.

2 tablespoons extra virgin olive oil

1 pound shiitake mushrooms, stems removed, very roughly sliced

Maldon or other flaky salt

Freshly ground black pepper

4 ounces linguine or similar pasta

¼ red onion, finely chopped

2 garlic cloves, minced

½ bottle pale ale (the rest is to drink)

2 tablespoons crème fraîche, optional

¾ cup freshly grated Parmesan cheese

1 small handful fresh flat-leaf parsley leaves

1. Heat 1 tablespoon olive oil in a large sauté pan over high heat until smoking hot. Add the mushrooms and a good pinch of salt and pepper. Cook for 5 to 6 minutes, until the mushrooms get some good color, stirring every now and then. This strong sear will give the mushrooms a good flavor, so don't be tempted to turn the heat down.

2. Meanwhile, bring a large saucepan of water to a boil. Cook the pasta according to the package directions to al dente.

3. Next, turn the heat under the mushrooms to low and let the pan cool for 2 to 3 minutes, then add the onion, garlic, and the remaining 1 tablespoon olive oil. Note: Don't rush and add them when the pan's

too hot or they'll burn and ruin the dish. Cook for another 4 minutes or so, then turn the heat up to medium-high, add the pale ale, and let it cook away and reduce slightly, leaving some liquid in the pan. Turn the heat off and, if using it, stir in the crème fraîche.

4. Using a pair of tongs, pull the al dente pasta out of the cooking water and place it directly in the pan with the mushroom mixture. Give it a good toss and serve topped with the Parmesan.

israeli couscous with shrimp and zucchini

{ Serves 4 to 6 }

The lemon, cumin, and fresh herbs combined with the richness of the shrimp and the great texture of the Israeli couscous make this wonderful eating. Be sure to taste the dish before serving to check that it has enough seasoning and lemon—it'll make the meal.

1½ pounds uncooked shrimp

2 cups uncooked Israeli couscous

2 cups grated zucchini (1½ to 2 zucchinis)

2 to 3 garlic cloves, minced

¼ red onion, finely chopped

3 whole scallions, thinly sliced

2 tablespoons extra virgin olive oil

1 tablespoon ground cumin

Juice of 1 lemon, plus more as needed

Agave nectar

Maldon or other flaky salt

Freshly ground black pepper

1 large handful fresh cilantro leaves

1 large handful fresh flat-leaf parsley leaves

1 handful fresh dill leaves (no big stems)

1. Bring a large pot of salted water to a boil. Add the shrimp and cook for about 1 minute, until pink. (The exact time will depend on their size, but be careful not to overcook them.) Remove the shrimp with a slotted spoon and run cold water over them to stop the cooking.

2. Keep the water boiling and add the couscous. Cook for 8 to 10 minutes, until al dente.

3. While the couscous is cooking, place the zucchini in a bowl and add the garlic, red onion, scallions, and shrimp.

4. Drain the couscous and run it under cold water to stop the cooking. Shake off as much excess water as possible and add the couscous to the bowl with the zucchini.

5. Add the olive oil, cumin, lemon juice, and a squeeze of agave nectar; season with salt and pepper. Give it a good mix and check the seasoning. Add the herbs and mix again. Recheck the seasoning, adding more lemon juice if necessary.

crab, tomato, and lemon spaghetti

{ Serves 4 }

The use of plain yogurt in this pasta makes for a healthier sauce than a cream-based one, and it adds an interesting depth and flavor to the dish.

2 tablespoons extra virgin olive oil

2 tablespoons finely chopped red onion

1 or 2 garlic cloves, minced

8 ounces spaghetti (or any other pasta)

2 cups picked fresh crabmeat

3 tomatoes, seeded and sliced

⅔ cup plain yogurt

½ lemon

Maldon or other flaky salt

Freshly ground black pepper

1 handful fresh flat-leaf parsley leaves

1. Heat the olive oil in a sauté pan over low heat. Add the onion and garlic and sweat for about 4 minutes, until softened but without color.

2. Meanwhile, bring a saucepan of salted water to a boil and cook the spaghetti according to the package directions, then drain, reserving a scoopful of the cooking liquid.

3. Add the crab and tomatoes to the sauté pan and gently sauté for 5 minutes over very low heat. Stir in the yogurt and remove from the heat. Season with a good squeeze of lemon and some salt and pepper. Give it a taste and adjust the seasoning if necessary.

4. Add the pasta to the pan, along with a tablespoon of the cooking water to keep the sauce from getting too sticky. Add the parsley and serve.

NOTE: *See page 98 for photos of seeding tomatoes.*

green herb and lemon zest gnocchi

{ Serves 4 }

Sometimes it can't all be whole grains and leaves, and on those occasions, this is the type of food I like to eat. Gnocchi when it's made well is light and beautiful, and I find the texture so comforting. This is a great little dish to serve when entertaining a few friends—it seems impressive to have made the effort, but it's pretty easy.

I could happily eat a huge bowl of this served with a simple arugula salad, but it's wonderful with so many different sauces. You could serve it as I have here just lightly tossed in some olive oil when it's finished, or you could toss it in some Arugula and Walnut Pesto (page 273) or, as I really, really love it, with Tomato Pesto (page 293).

3 large russet potatoes	1 small handful basil, finely chopped
1 teaspoon plus 1 tablespoon olive oil	1 small handful parsley, finely chopped
Heaping ½ cup all-purpose flour	Maldon or other flaky salt
1 small egg yolk	Freshly ground black pepper
Zest from 1 lemon	Grated Parmesan, for serving

1. Preheat the oven to 400°F.

2. Use a fork to prick a few holes in each potato and rub each potato with a little of the olive oil. Place the potatoes on a baking sheet and bake them for just over an hour, or until the skin is crispy and the inside is soft (you're basically just making baked potatoes).

3. Scoop the flesh from each potato and pass it through a sieve set over

a large bowl. (This is called "ricing"—some people use a ricer, but a sieve will work just fine for this; if you want to impress people with light, smooth mashed potatoes, this is how to do it, by the way.)

4. Add the flour, egg yolk, lemon zest, herbs, salt, and pepper to the potatoes and combine. Taste the mixture at this point to test the seasoning. (It may be a little lemony, but that'll calm down when it's cooked—you're only testing for seasoning at this point.)

5. Use your hands to work the mixture together—the best gnocchi are light, so don't overwork the dough—about 30 seconds is right—but it is important that it's well blended. You'll know it's done when you have a mixture that holds together when you make a ball out of it. Test a piece on your clean countertop—if it sticks or falls apart, add just a little flour.

6. Take a handful of the mixture and roll it into a sausage shape on your counter. When it is about as wide as an average thumb, use a knife to cut it into 1-inch pieces. Then, using a fork, make little indentations in the top. (This helps the gnocchi pick up any sauce or olive oil they're served with, and it'll make you look like a pro.) Repeat with the rest of the mixture.

7. Dust a baking sheet with flour and spread the gnocchi on it. Refrigerate for about 5 minutes to chill and firm up the gnocchi.

8. Bring a large pot of salted water to a boil. Drop the gnocchi in the water. They will take about 2 minutes to cook; they'll tell you when they're done because they'll pop to the surface.

9. Heat a sauté pan with 1 tablespoon extra virgin olive oil. Drain the gnocchi and add them to the hot pan. Carefully toss around in the hot oil for about 30 seconds and serve immediately, topped with a little grated Parmesan.

Fish market, Borneo.

Seafood

asian lobster tails

{ Serves 2 to 4 }

Cooking in paper is a great way to prepare lobster, but you can also make this recipe with shrimp—just reduce the cooking time depending on their size. I love serving this at a dinner party. Make 1 package per guest and take them all out to the table on a tray. When everyone starts opening their packages, the smell is incredible!

To mix it up, use different types of seafood in each bag. Some people will get mussels, others lobster, and others prawns. Then they can swap them all around and share. This is perfect served with Lime and Cilantro Rice (page 250), or with a side of noodles.

The shellfish can be made in the oven on a small baking sheet, but the paper packets are more fun—plus, you have no baking sheet to clean.

Equipment: kitchen twine

1 lemongrass stalk, halved, green parts only

1 to 1½ red serrano chiles, sliced

8 black peppercorns

2 scallions, thinly sliced

1 thumb-size piece ginger, sliced

2 garlic cloves, sliced

2 tablespoons minced fresh cilantro stalks

Maldon or other flaky salt

Freshly ground black pepper

A few slices of lime

A few splashes of fish sauce, optional

4 small lobster tails, about 5 ounces each, halved with scissors (see photo, page 144)

1 cup coconut milk

Fresh basil leaves, optional

Fresh mint leaves, optional

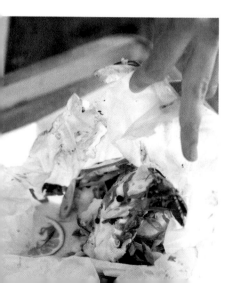

1. Preheat the oven to 400°F.

2. In a large bowl, combine the lemongrass, chiles, peppercorns, scallions, ginger, garlic, and cilantro. Season with salt, pepper, and lime and a few splashes of fish sauce.

3. Place 2 pieces of wax paper over 2 ovenproof bowls. Fill each one with half of the mixture and arrange 4 pieces of lobster on top. Pour ½ cup of the coconut milk into each package. Tie the packages with kitchen twine and bake them for 15 to 20 minutes. When the lobster tails are cooked, the shells will turn a beautiful coral color that you can see through the paper. You really don't want the lobster to be overcooked, so after 15 minutes, open up a package to check how it's going.

4. Garnish with fresh basil and mint and serve in the paper, or with a side of rice or noodles.

Variation

mediterranean lobster tails

This adaptation of the Asian Lobster Tails recipe uses the same method and can also be made with either mussels or shrimp in different packets. It's really wonderful served with Garlic Bread Stuffed with Italian Herbs (page 257) so that you can mop up all the beautiful juices from the seafood.

Simply substitute 2 tablespoons capers for the lemongrass, chiles, ginger, and cilantro; ⅔ cup sauvignon blanc or other dry white wine for the coconut milk; a sliced half lemon for the lime; and a couple of dill sprigs for the mint.

Mediterranean Lobster Tails.

cornmeal squid with avocado and yogurt sauce

{ Serves 4 }

I know a lot of people don't like squid, or the idea of it, but I think that's unfair. In fact, most people love fried calamari, and this is a sort of variation on that. It's very easy to make, and definitely worth a try.

1 pound squid, cleaned (see photos)

3 cups vegetable oil, for frying

½ cup all-purpose flour, for dusting

Maldon or other flaky salt

Freshly ground black pepper

2 eggs

½ cup cornmeal, for dusting

½ tablespoon ground turmeric

Avocado and Yogurt Dipping Sauce (page 277)

Fresh cilantro sprigs, for garnish

1. Clean the squid and cut it into bite-size pieces (see photos).

2. Heat the oil in a saucepan over medium-high heat.

3. Set up 3 bowls to dust and dredge the squid before frying. In the first bowl, combine the flour with salt and pepper to taste. In the second bowl, beat the eggs lightly. In the third bowl, mix the cornmeal and turmeric.

4. Working in small batches, dredge the squid in the flour mixture, then dip it in the egg and coat it with the cornmeal mixture.

5. When the oil is hot enough (see Note), still working in batches, carefully drop the squid into the oil and let it cook for 20 seconds. Use a slotted spoon to remove the squid and drain it on paper towels.

6. Serve over Avocado and Yogurt Sauce and topped with a few sprigs of cilantro.

NOTE: *To test the oil to see whether it's ready, drop a tiny bit of cornmeal into the saucepan. If it bubbles, the oil is ready.*

fish tacos

{ Serves 2 to 4 }

I know, I know, everybody has their version of a fish taco. But I've included mine here because I've gotten so much positive feedback on it. It's super-simple and full of zesty lime.

If you don't feel like a taco, the tasty fish mixture can be eaten by itself with a side salad, or even served on top of Lime and Cilantro Rice (page 250).

Extra virgin olive oil

¼ red onion, thinly sliced

1 tablespoon minced fresh cilantro stems

½ tablespoon ground cumin

½ tablespoon ground coriander

1 tomato, roughly chopped

12 ounces tilapia or snapper (or ask the fishmonger to recommend something similar), cubed

1 garlic clove, minced

2 scallions, thinly sliced

Maldon or other flaky salt

Freshly ground black pepper

Juice of 1½ limes

1 large handful fresh cilantro leaves

6 small flour tortillas

1. Get a skillet very hot over high heat and add 2 tablespoons olive oil. Add the onion and sauté for about 4 minutes, allowing it to brown slightly but not burn.

2. Reduce the heat to medium and add the cilantro stems, cumin, and coriander. Sauté for a couple of minutes to toast the spices, then add the tomato, fish, and garlic. Sauté for about 2 minutes, until the fish

is done (you'll see when it's done when it's just turned white and falls apart to the touch). Add the scallions, salt and pepper to taste, the lime juice, and cilantro leaves. Give a final gentle toss, taking care not to crush the fish. Check the seasoning and serve with tortillas. Make sure there's enough lime in the dish; it'll lift the whole thing.

green quinoa–crusted bass

{ Serves 4 }

I love the idea of a crust or topping on a fish like this, but I don't like the thought of that crust being filled with bread crumbs and butter, so this is my healthier version. Eating fish is good for you, and using quinoa in this recipe makes the dish even healthier.

This is another one of those dishes that looks like a lot more effort than it is. The first time around, you'll need to follow the pictures and read through the recipe, but afterward you'll whip it up quickly. It's great for a dinner party because you can prep the fish hours in advance and keep it covered in the refrigerator. Just bring it out about 20 minutes before you put it in the oven so that it's not fridge-cold.

¼ cup pine nuts

¼ cup uncooked quinoa

1 garlic clove, minced

Zest of ½ lemon

Extra virgin olive oil

2 cups tightly packed fresh green herbs (a mix of parsley, dill, mint, cilantro, and basil)

Maldon or other flaky salt

Freshly ground black pepper

Four 4-ounce boneless, skinless pieces of bass

Tomato and Leek Sauce (page 267)

1. Toast the pine nuts in a small dry skillet over low heat for about 2 minutes, until lightly browned. Watch carefully so that they don't burn.

2. Cook the quinoa in boiling water for about 15 minutes and drain. Place it back in the dry saucepan over low heat and stir for 1 minute to remove excess water. Remove from the heat and let cool.

3. Add the quinoa to a blender with the garlic, pine nuts, lemon zest, ¼ cup olive oil, herbs, and salt and pepper to taste. Blend until it forms a smooth paste. Check the seasoning and adjust as necessary (see photos, pages 154–155).

4. Lay some plastic wrap flat on a clean work surface and spoon the mixture onto the plastic wrap. Top with another layer of plastic wrap. Using a rolling pin, roll the mixture into a rough rectangle that's about ¼ inch thick. This will be your crust. Place it on a plate in the fridge to stiffen up for about 30 minutes.

5. Preheat the oven to 450°F.

6. Remove the crust from the fridge and place it on the work surface again. Peel off the top layer of plastic wrap and discard it. Then, using a knife, cut out 4 pieces of the crust to match the size of your fish. Rub the fish in a bit of olive oil. Use a spatula to pick up the crust pieces and place them on top of the fish.

7. Season the bottom of a baking sheet with salt, pepper, and a drizzle of olive oil and place the pieces of fish on the sheet.

8. Bake the fish for about 5 minutes, until cooked to your liking. Serve on top of Tomato and Leek Sauce.

herb, lemon, and caper-stuffed trout

{ Serves 2 to 4 }

This is a very simple way to cook fish. You can use snapper, bass, bronzini—they'll all work well. Simply adjust the time accordingly.

2 whole trout, about 12 ounces each, descaled

2 handfuls fresh herbs (such as dill, parsley, or cilantro)

About 6 lemon slices

3 heaping tablespoons capers

Maldon or other flaky salt

Freshly ground black pepper

A few lugs of extra virgin olive oil

1. Preheat the oven to 375°F.

2. Using kitchen scissors, cut off the fins of the trout to neaten them up and so they don't burn.

3. Stuff the fish with the herbs, lemon slices, and capers. Season the inside of the fish with salt and pepper and add a drizzle of olive oil.

4. Place the fish on a baking sheet, drizzle some olive oil over the top of the fish, then season well with salt and pepper.

5. Pop in the oven for about 12 minutes, depending on the size. To test for doneness, remove the fish and give the flesh a pinch with your pointer finger and thumb—if it flakes easily, it's cooked; if not, return to the oven for a few more minutes.

lobster quinoa

{ Serves 6 }

This is another DVF favorite—it's so luxurious and fresh.

When I'm aboard *Eos,* I'm often approached by fishermen in little boats carrying huge whole lobsters. Cooking lobster sometimes can be daunting because it might seem like a massive effort to buy and prepare the whole thing. When I'm on land, I usually just buy the tails, so I'd recommend you try that too.

The horseradish is the secret weapon in this quinoa, so definitely make sure to get some, even for just a small amount. You can add more if you like an extra kick. (I do!)

You could buy cooked lobster tails if you don't want to get into cooking them—in that case, start at step 3.

6 lobster tails, shell on, cut in half with kitchen scissors

Extra virgin olive oil

¼ cup sauvignon blanc or other dry white wine

1 fresh dill sprig

Maldon or other flaky salt

Freshly ground black pepper

2 heaping cups uncooked quinoa

1 cup cherry tomatoes, halved

¼ cup good-quality mayonnaise (see Note)

2 garlic cloves, minced

¼ red onion, finely chopped

4 teaspoons jarred prepared horseradish (not the sauce)

Tabasco sauce (just a few shakes or a lot of shakes)

Juice of 1 lemon

1 handful fresh mint leaves, roughly chopped

1 handful fresh dill sprigs, roughly chopped (no big stems)

1 handful fresh flat-leaf parsley, roughly chopped

Squeeze of agave nectar

1. If you're not using cooked lobster tails, preheat the oven to 350°F.

2. Place the lobster tails, olive oil, wine, dill, and salt and pepper to taste in a foil pouch. Bake for about 20 minutes, checking after 15 minutes, until the lobster is just cooked through and opaque in the middle. Let cool.

3. Cook the quinoa in boiling water for 15 minutes and drain. Return to the saucepan over low heat; stir for 1 minute with a wooden spoon to remove the excess water.

4. Place the warm quinoa in a large glass bowl and mix in the tomatoes, mayonnaise, garlic, onion, horseradish, Tabasco, and lemon juice.

5. While the lobster is still warm, add it to the quinoa, gently breaking up the lobster meat into manageable-size pieces. (If you have precooked lobster, break it up and add it here.) Mix in the herbs so that they all fuse together nicely and the flavors meld. The rough edges of the lobster will help it soak up the other flavors.

6. Set aside to cool to room temperature or cover and refrigerate until you're ready to serve. Just before serving, add some more lemon juice, salt, pepper, and agave to balance.

NOTE: *I don't use a lot of mayonnaise, but when I do, I use Kewpie mayonnaise. It's the best for cooking because it's mild and smooth and not too fatty or thick. It's a Japanese product, but it's getting easier and easier to find at grocery stores or specialty shops, and I like the packaging!*

poached salmon with shrimp served on couscous

{ Serves 4 to 6 }

Poaching is a wonderful way to cook fish because it's completely gentle and stress-free, so the result is a beautifully delicate piece of fish. This dish is full of its own natural flavor because the salmon poaching liquid is used to cook the shrimp and couscous. It's also a really easy dish to make and great for a dinner party when you want to make it seem special but not have to do too much.

I love to serve this dish with a very simple but delicious Avocado, Arugula, and Spinach Salad (page 102), but it can go with anything you like.

½ bottle good sauvignon blanc or other white wine

2-pound side of wild salmon (ask your fishmonger to debone a side, and skin it too, if you like)

2 garlic cloves, roughly crushed with the back of a knife

1 handful fresh dill leaves

1 handful fresh parsley leaves

½ Meyer lemon, cut into wedges

Maldon or other flaky salt

Freshly ground black pepper

Extra virgin olive oil

½ pound shrimp, shelled and deveined

1 heaping cup uncooked couscous

Zest of 1 lemon

1 handful mixed fresh herb leaves (such as parsley, dill, and mint), three-quarters roughly chopped and one-quarter reserved for garnish

1. Preheat the oven to 300°F.

2. To make the poaching liquid, pour the wine and ½ cup water into a baking dish large enough to hold the salmon and add the garlic, dill, parsley, and lemon wedges. Season with salt and pepper and give it a little taste to make sure you can taste the salt.

3. Place the salmon in the baking dish. It should be almost completely submerged, though if a bit of the surface is exposed, it's fine. Drizzle a little olive oil over the top and season with a little more salt and pepper. Bake for 10 to 12 minutes, until the fish looks about halfway cooked.

4. Add the shrimp to the baking dish and make sure they are fully submerged around the salmon, then return the dish to the oven for another 8 minutes or so. Important: You don't want to overcook the shrimp. You'll know they're cooked when they become opaque instead of translucent, but if you're not sure, take one out and pull it in half to check. Just remember that it should be delicately poached and tender when it's done, not undercooked and certainly not tough. As for the salmon, I like mine a little rare in the middle, but you can cook yours through; just take special care not to overcook. The easiest way to test for doneness is to pull the salmon out of the oven and gently press down on the middle of the fillet with your fingertips. When it's perfectly done, it will give way in the shape of flakes. Raw feels, well, raw, and overcooked feels firm and tight. When it just starts to fall apart from a gentle prod, you're good.

5. Remove the baking dish from the oven, take ½ cup of the beautiful hot poaching liquid, and add it to a bowl with the couscous. Cover the salmon with aluminum foil to keep it warm, and cover the couscous

with plastic wrap. Let the couscous sit for 5 minutes, or until all the liquid is absorbed and the couscous is tender. Fluff the couscous with your fingertips and add the lemon zest and the chopped mixed herbs.

6. To serve, spread the couscous out on a serving platter and carefully place the salmon in the middle of the plate. The trick is to lift the salmon out slowly! If possible, ask someone to help you by using a couple of spatulas and working together. To finish off the dish, spoon over some of the extra poaching liquid and garnish with the remaining herb leaves and the cooked Meyer lemon wedges.

NOTE: *If you're not going to eat the salmon with the couscous, let the fish cool down a little in the stock and then lift it out onto a platter. Throw some fresh herbs over the top and serve. Or cool, refrigerate for up to a couple of days, and serve it flaked on a salad or pasta.*

south african pickled fish

{ Serves 4 }

This is a very typical Cape Malay dish from Cape Town, where I grew up. The food in the region is heavily influenced by the Malay people, who used to pickle their fish as a way to preserve them.

Pickled fish is a traditional dish at Easter and is best served with warm crusty white bread.

Extra virgin olive oil

1 tablespoon ground turmeric

½ tablespoon curry powder

2 garlic cloves, thinly sliced

2 tablespoons thinly sliced fresh ginger

8 peppercorns

1 bay leaf

½ white onion, cut into rings

1½ cups white vinegar

½ cup agave nectar or ¾ to 1 cup sugar

1 tablespoon Maldon or other flaky salt

1 pound firm-fleshed white fish, such as arctic char

All-purpose flour seasoned with salt and pepper for dusting, plus 1 teaspoon flour for thickening

Fresh cilantro sprigs, optional

1. Heat a lug of olive oil in a medium saucepan over low heat. Add the turmeric, curry powder, garlic, ginger, peppercorns, and bay leaf and stir for a few minutes. The smell of the spices toasting will fill the house, so open some windows if you can. This first step lets the spices gently toast by themselves, which releases all the goodness in them. Add the onion and cook for a couple more minutes, until the rings are soft, taking care not to let the spices burn.

2. Add the vinegar, ½ cup water, the agave nectar, and salt to the saucepan and gently simmer for about 15 minutes, until it's thickened and has become a little viscous.

3. Meanwhile, get a skillet hot and add a little olive oil. Dredge the fish well in the seasoned flour. Fry the fish for a few minutes on each side; it is done when the flesh is tender to the touch. Prod it gently with your finger, and if it looks like it could push apart in flakes, it's done. Set aside.

4. Pour the spice-vinegar liquid into a baking dish and carefully place the fish in it. Make sure that the fish is fully submerged in the liquid and covered with the onion and garlic pieces.

5. Cover and refrigerate for at least 2 days.

6. When the fish is pickled and ready, serve it with cilantro, if you like.

tuna and udon noodles
with ginger dressing

{ Serves 2 to 4 }

This is a lovely summery lunch dish. It can be served as a meal for two, or you could double it up and serve it to a group with an Asian slaw alongside.

4 ounces udon noodles

Sesame oil

1 garlic clove, minced

1 large thumb-size piece ginger, minced (preferably over a bowl to catch the juices)

⅓ cup soy sauce

1 tablespoon agave nectar

3 scallions, thinly sliced on the diagonal

1 small handful fresh mint leaves, very roughly chopped, plus sprigs, for garnish

1 handful fresh cilantro leaves, roughly chopped, plus sprigs, for garnish

½ pound sushi-grade tuna

2 radishes, thinly sliced and crisped in ice water, for garnish

1 lime, neatly quartered, seeds removed

2 tablespoons black sesame seeds, optional

1. Cook the udon noodles according to the package directions. Drain and toss with a little sesame oil to stop them from sticking and set aside.

2. In a glass bowl, combine the garlic, ginger, soy sauce, agave nectar, scallions, and noodles. Give the mixture a good toss, then add the mint and cilantro leaves.

3. Get a skillet very hot and add a good lug or two of sesame oil. Add the tuna to the pan, giving it a shake back and forth for the first

minute or so to prevent it from sticking. How long you cook the tuna really depends on how you like it. I like a quick 20 seconds on each side, so it's colored on the outside and nice and rare in the middle, but it's up to you.

4. When the tuna is cooked, let it sit on a cutting board for a minute or so. While the tuna is resting, lift the noodles onto a plate and dress with some of the sauce. Cut the tuna into thick slices and arrange them on top of the noodles. Spoon over any leftover sauce and garnish with cilantro and mint sprigs and radish slices. Top with a couple of lime quarters, and if you like, sprinkle with the sesame seeds.

shrimp with citrus sweet potato

{ Serves 3 to 4 }

This dish reminds me of something similar I tasted in a restaurant in New York. I loved the idea of citrus with sweet potato. This is a really great dish to do on a large platter and serve in the middle of the table.

1 pound sweet potatoes, peeled and cut into 1-inch pieces

Extra virgin olive oil

Maldon or other flaky salt

Freshly ground black pepper

2 teaspoons agave nectar

2 teaspoons minced fresh ginger

½ garlic clove, minced

2 limes (1 for juice and 1 for wedges)

1 orange

2 pounds medium shrimp, peeled and deveined

3 ounces bay scallops

Leaves from ⅓ bunch fresh cilantro

1. Preheat the oven to 400°F.

2. Place the sweet potatoes on a piece of aluminum foil. Coat with olive oil and season with salt and pepper. Add a drizzle of agave nectar and give it a quick toss to coat the sweet potato pieces. Seal the foil into a package and roast the sweet potatoes for about 40 minutes, until they are bright orange and soft to the touch but not mushy.

3. Tip the sweet potatoes into a glass bowl, along with any juices that might have collected in the bottom of the aluminum foil. This will be a wonderfully tasty oil, so don't waste any of it.

4. With the back of a fork, crush the sweet potatoes to create a rough mash. Add the ginger and garlic. Squeeze in the juice of half a lime and half the orange, season with salt and pepper, and adjust the seasonings as desired. Set aside to bring to room temperature.

5. Throw the shrimp into a smoking hot skillet, and season with salt and pepper. Cook for about a minute on each side, depending on the size of the shrimp. You want to get some color on the shrimp, so the pan really needs to be hot, but be careful not to overcook the shrimp—remember that they'll continue to cook once you've taken them out of the pan.

6. When the shrimp are cooked halfway through, throw in the scallops. Cook until they are opaque in the middle—this should only take a minute or so. Near the end of the cooking, add a small squeeze of lime juice and orange juice. Warning: It'll give off quite a bit of smoke—just be sure to keep the pan moving and you'll create some really great flavors in that hot pan.

7. Put the sweet potatoes on a plate and top with the shrimp and scallops. Pour any pan juices on top. Tear some fresh cilantro leaves over the top and garnish with a couple of lime wedges.

cilantro fish

{ Serves 4 }

Bass is a beautiful fish, so I try not to do too much to it. One of my favorite things about it is its delicate texture, so I cook it in the oven—which is more gentle—rather than in a frying pan. This is best served over Tamarind and Coconut Lentils.

marinade

1 teaspoon minced ginger

1 garlic clove, minced

Zest of ½ lime

1½ handfuls fresh cilantro leaves

3 to 4 tablespoons extra virgin olive oil

Maldon or other flaky salt

Squeeze of agave nectar

Four 4-ounce pieces of boneless, skinless bass

Tamarind and Coconut Lentils (page 265)

1. Preheat the oven to 400°F.

2. Combine all the marinade ingredients in a blender and blend until completely smooth. Check the seasoning.

3. Lay the fish in a baking dish and top with the marinade. Using your hands, gently toss the fish in the sauce so that it's distributed evenly.

4. Bake for about 6 minutes, until cooked to your liking. Be sure to check halfway through to see how it's going! Serve on top of Tamarind and Coconut Lentils.

ecuadorian-inspired ceviche

{ Serves 2 or 3 }

Ceviche is something I crave every now and then. It's sharp and vibrant and gets my taste buds going.

I spent a couple of days in mainland Ecuador looking for food suppliers while *Eos* was in the Galápagos Islands. I was by myself in Quito, which is notoriously dangerous, wandering the streets going from market to market. I made it out safe and sound, and although it wasn't a comfortable experience, I'm grateful for the ceviche I ate there.

Ecuadorians add ketchup to their ceviche, which sounds terrible, but a little bit makes an already good dish more interesting. In my recipe it's almost undetectable after the two hours in the fridge, but it makes a difference. I think you should give it a try, but make sure you use only the very best quality ketchup. If you don't have that, then you can leave it out of the recipe.

10 ounces striped bass (you could use halibut, or another type of bass, if you like), diced into ½-inch pieces

2 lemons

2 tomatoes, seeded and neatly diced

2 tablespoons finely chopped red onion

1 teaspoon agave nectar

1 handful cilantro, roughly chopped

1 small garlic clove, minced

1 teaspoon minced fresh ginger

1 tablespoon chopped mint

1½ teaspoons best-quality ketchup (optional)

Maldon or other flaky salt

Tortilla chips, for serving (optional)

Combine all the ingredients in a nonreactive bowl and refrigerate for at least 2 hours and up to 24 hours. When you're ready to serve, give it a good mix around and check your seasoning. I like to eat ceviche with good-quality tortilla chips.

CURCUMIN

Meat

beef tagliata with chopped arugula and basil salad

{ Serves 4 to 6 }

This recipe makes my mouth water. It's simple in execution and ingredients, but it's so good and will appeal to anyone. The chopped salad is basically a pesto but kept rough, which works best with the grilled meat. To avoid the expense of a big tenderloin, you could serve this with any piece of grilled meat, particularly beef.

One 5-pound beef tenderloin

1 tablespoon extra virgin olive oil, plus more for coating the tenderloin

Maldon or other flaky salt

Freshly ground black pepper

½ cup pine nuts

1 garlic clove, minced

¾ cup freshly grated Parmesan cheese

3 handfuls arugula, very roughly chopped

2 handfuls fresh basil leaves, very roughly chopped

Freshly grated lemon zest

1. Preheat the oven to 450°F.

2. Rub the tenderloin with olive oil to coat, then a generous amount of salt and pepper. Place it in a smoking hot ovenproof skillet and brown all sides of the beef, a couple of minutes on each side. Set the skillet in the oven to roast the beef for about 20 minutes—15 if the meat is a bit shy of 5 pounds. This cut of meat is really best served rare to medium rare, but allow more time to cook it if you like it more well done.

3. Meanwhile, in a small dry skillet over medium-low heat, toast the pine nuts for 2 to 3 minutes, until golden, stirring often and taking care that they don't burn. Lightly crush the pine nuts and set them aside to cool.

4. Remove the beef from the oven and transfer to a cutting board; cover in foil and allow the meat to rest for at least 15 minutes.

5. Meanwhile, to make the salad, combine the pine nuts, garlic, Parmesan, arugula, basil, 1 tablespoon olive oil, and lemon zest. Season with salt and pepper.

6. To serve, slice the beef and spread it out on a platter. Dress it with the chopped arugula and basil salad.

cape malay lamb curry

{ Serves 4 }

The food in South Africa is really diverse, and there's a big Malay influence in Cape Town, where I'm from, which results in dishes that are wonderfully spiced and fragrant. This is my version of a Cape Malay curry. I serve it with Cardamom Rice and Pineapple and Chile Relish, and it's also great with finely diced banana scattered over the curry. It may sound strange, but it's a great little addition, and something I remember so clearly from eating my grandmother's curry.

2 pounds lamb stew meat, cut into 1-inch chunks

Maldon or other flaky salt

Freshly ground black pepper

Extra virgin olive oil

½ red onion, roughly chopped

3 garlic cloves, minced

1 thumb-size piece ginger, minced

2 teaspoons ground turmeric

2 tablespoons ground coriander

2 tablespoons curry powder

1 tablespoon ground cumin

⅓ cup finely chopped fresh cilantro stems

1 bay leaf

1 cinnamon stick

About 5 peppercorns

Zest and juice of 1 lemon

Two 14.5-ounce cans diced tomatoes

1 large handful fresh cilantro leaves

Agave nectar

Cardamom Rice (page 260)

Pineapple and Chile Relish (page 284)

1. Preheat the oven to 350°F. Place the lamb in a medium bowl and toss with some salt and pepper.

2. Get a Dutch oven very hot on the stovetop. When it's just smoking, add a lug of olive oil and the lamb, working in batches so that the pieces of lamb don't touch (or they will stew, not brown). Sear the lamb on all sides for at least 10 minutes, until beautifully brown. This stage is very important—it will add lots of flavor. Remove the lamb from the pot and turn the heat down a little.

3. Add the onion and cook for about 5 minutes, until browned, but don't let it burn. Keep the onion pieces moving to pick up some of the brown from the meat and to develop their sweetness. Reduce the heat to low and cook for 1 minute, then add the garlic, ginger, turmeric, coriander, curry, cumin, cilantro stems, bay leaf, cinnamon, peppercorns, and lemon zest. Stir for a few minutes to form a paste and toast the spices.

4. Add the tomatoes, 1½ cups water, and salt to taste. Cover and place in the oven. Cook the curry for 1 hour, then remove the pot and stir. If there is a lot of liquid still remaining, keep the pot uncovered to let some of those juices go; otherwise, keep it covered. Return to the oven to cook for 30 minutes, or until the lamb is starting to fall apart.

5. Let the pot sit off the heat for about 15 minutes to allow the meat to rest and settle. Stir in the cilantro, a squeeze of agave nectar, and the lemon juice. Serve with Cardamom Rice and Pineapple and Chile Relish.

chicken and beef koftas

{ Serves 4 }

These are delicious. A kofta is basically the Middle Eastern version of a meatball. I've included a couple versions of them, so you can see how easy to make and tasty they are. Play around with the different methods and ingredients, and try mixing it up to see what you like best. I can safely say that koftas make a lot of people happy, so it's worth adding them to your repertoire.

I serve these with Spinach, Pomegranate, Dill, and Cilantro Chopped Salad.

½ pound ground beef

½ pound ground organic, free-range chicken

2 teaspoons ground cumin

2 teaspoons ground coriander

⅓ cup chopped fresh cilantro

Zest of ½ lemon

3 tablespoons chopped red onion

1 large garlic clove, minced

1 egg yolk

Maldon or other flaky salt

Freshly ground black pepper

3 ounces feta cheese, crumbled

2 tablespoons canola oil

Spinach, Pomegranate, Dill, and Cilantro Chopped Salad (page 106)

1. Put the beef, chicken, cumin, coriander, cilantro, lemon zest, onion, and garlic in a large glass bowl and mix well with your hands (hands are really the best mixers here). Add the egg yolk, a couple of good pinches of salt, and pepper to taste and mix again. Add the feta and gently mix it in. Wrap the mixture with plastic wrap and refrigerate for at least 10 minutes or up to 2 hours.

2. Remove the meat from the fridge and form it into elongated meatballs, kind of like the shape of a football, or any shape you like. I use about 2 tablespoons of the meat mixture per meatball.

3. Heat the oil in a sauté pan over medium-high heat until the pan is very hot. Working in batches if necessary, add the meatballs to the hot pan and cook them on all sides for about 3 minutes total. They'll taste so much better with some good color on them, so shake the pan around to brown them evenly on all sides. Remove them from the pan and place in aluminum foil to form a parcel. Pop them in the oven for another 5 minutes to finish them off.

4. Serve with Spinach, Pomegranate, Dill, and Cilantro Chopped Salad.

chicken stew with lemon and a side of israeli couscous

{ Serves 3 }

This stew is always a hit. It's very, very simple but so comforting and full of flavor, and I like the texture of the Israeli couscous with it.

One of my favorite guests on the boat, Antonia, used to love when I made her a little chicken potpie. Try using this stew as a potpie mix. Just place it in a baking dish or little ramekins and cover with some good-quality puff pastry. Brush with some egg wash (beaten egg with milk) and pop in a 400°F oven till golden brown. That's love in a baking dish.

6 boneless, skinless organic chicken thighs

Maldon or other flaky salt

Freshly ground black pepper

Extra virgin olive oil

Just under ¼ cup all-purpose flour

1 cup sauvignon blanc or other white wine

4 ounces shiitake mushrooms, stems removed, roughly chopped

6 ounces button mushrooms, roughly chopped

½ red onion, finely chopped

4 celery stalks, chopped

2 garlic cloves, grated on a Microplane

1 bay leaf

2 fresh thyme sprigs

2 cups uncooked Israeli couscous

Lemon zest

Juice of ½ lemon

1 large handful fresh flat-leaf parsley leaves, roughly chopped

1 small handful fresh dill, roughly chopped

1 large handful baby cress or baby spinach

1. Slice half the chicken thighs into 6 pieces and the other half into 3 pieces. In stews I like having different-size pieces of meat, as it adds a nice texture. Place the chicken into a large bowl and season well with salt and pepper.

2. Heat 2 tablespoons olive oil in a large saucepan or Dutch oven over high heat. When it's very hot, add the chicken. You want it to be really hot so that the chicken gets lovely and brown in parts. When the chicken pieces have colored a little, turn the heat off, put the chicken back into the bowl, add the flour, and toss to coat.

3. Add the wine to your original pot and use a wooden spoon to get all the pieces off the bottom of the pot. Pour this mixture over the flour-coated chicken pieces.

4. Using the same pan over high heat, add another lug of olive oil. When it's smoking hot, add the mushrooms. Again, you want them to color slightly, to bring out the best of their flavor. Cook for about 4 minutes, stirring occasionally. Don't add more oil, even if the mushrooms look dry at first (see Note), as they will soften in time.

5. Reduce the heat to low. When the pan has cooled a little, add the onion and celery and let them sweat down for about a minute, then add the garlic, bay leaf, and thyme. Cook for 3 to 4 minutes, until softened.

6. Add the chicken mixture, making sure you get everything out of the bowl, and 4 cups of water to the pan and season very lightly with salt and pepper. Bring to a simmer and simmer for about 1 hour, stirring occasionally.

7. In the meantime, place the Israeli couscous in a saucepan of salted boiling water and cook for 8 to 10 minutes, until al dente. Drain, add the zest, and season well.

8. The chicken will fall apart to the touch when it's ready, or if you like it to be more broken up, cook it longer—I like it so that it's only just able to hold itself together. Remove it from the heat, add the lemon juice, and season with salt and pepper. Add the parsley and dill.

9. Serve the chicken over the couscous and a handful of baby cress. I prefer cress because it's wonderfully peppery and fresh tasting, but if you can't find it, spinach works well, too.

NOTE: *Mushrooms are interesting because they're like little sponges—they soak up all the olive oil when they're being cooked. A common mistake is to saturate them because they do start out looking dry, but give them time— when they cook, they relax, and all that oil they soaked up will be released. So as tempting as it is to add oil, just let them be, and they'll keep their own flavor, rather than being overwhelmed by oil.*

chicken tagine

{ Serves 3 }

My Moroccan friend Naima taught me how to make this tagine. Her cooking is so wonderfully tasty, simple, and authentic, and this is a particularly great recipe.

2 tablespoons extra virgin olive oil

3 pounds boneless, skinless organic, free-range chicken thighs, cut in half

1 teaspoon ground turmeric

1 red onion, cut into 8 wedges

2 garlic cloves, minced

½ thumb-size piece ginger, minced

2 pinches saffron threads

Maldon or other flaky salt

One 15-ounce can chickpeas

⅓ cup green olives, pitted and halved

½ lemon

Agave nectar

½ cup roughly chopped fresh cilantro

½ cup roughly chopped fresh flat-leaf parsley

1. Heat the olive oil in a large saucepan until it's smoking hot. Add the chicken pieces and give them time to get some good color on each side, about 2 minutes, untouched, per side. Lower the heat to very low and wait a minute for the pan to cool a bit, then add the turmeric. Cook for a minute to toast the spice—you'll know when it's done toasting because you'll smell it (see Note).

2. Add the onion and stir for about a minute, then add the garlic, ginger, saffron, and a large pinch of salt. Add the chickpeas, including enough of their own liquid, to cover all the contents plus about an inch. Bring to a boil, then lower the heat to a simmer, cover partway with a lid, and cook for about 40 minutes, until you can see the

chicken has started to become more tender and the whole mixture looks thicker and comes together.

3. Remove the lid and give the stew a good stir. Simmer for another 15 minutes, stirring occasionally. If it looks as though the pot is too dry, you can add a bit of water.

4. Add the olives and cook for 5 minutes. Turn off the heat and let it sit for a few minutes to rest. Add the lemon juice and season with salt and agave, so that it's right for you. Finish with the cilantro and parsley.

NOTE: *Toasting a spice really brings out its flavor, and this recipe is a great use of the technique. Just take care not to burn the spices, or their flavor will be lost. When you're toasting spices, your nose will be the best way to tell when they're done. It's as if they suddenly burst with aroma. It sounds ridiculous, but I promise that you'll understand when you try it.*

moroccan lamb

{ Serves 4 }

One of the best meals I've ever had was at a restaurant in Marrakech called Dar Yacout. Course after course, the food was extraordinary. Toward the end of the meal, I had a lamb dish that really stuck out; I could taste the saffron and the ginger so clearly. This is my attempt to re-create that dish.

I serve this with steamed couscous and Beet and Orange Salad with a Citrus-Cumin Vinaigrette (page 111).

2 teaspoons ground cumin

2 teaspoons ground coriander

2 pounds lamb stew meat, cut into
    rough 1-inch chunks

Maldon or other flaky salt

2 tomatoes, quartered

1½ red onions, cut into 6 wedges, root
    intact

1 bouquet fresh parsley and cilantro
    (about 7 sprigs of each, tied together
    well with string)

1 thumb-size piece ginger, minced

2 garlic cloves

1 large pinch saffron

Freshly ground black pepper

Optional additions:

¼ butternut squash, peeled, seeded,
    and cut into 1-inch pieces

1 zucchini, quartered down the middle,
    then halved lengthwise

1 carrot, quartered down the middle,
    then halved lengthwise

Half to one 15-ounce can chickpeas,
    drained and rinsed

Lemon juice

Agave nectar

1. In a dry sauté pan over low heat, add the cumin and coriander. Cook for a few minutes, until fragrant and toasted. Set aside.

2. Place the lamb in a heavy-bottomed saucepan, sprinkle with salt,

give a quick toss, and let rest for 5 minutes. Add just enough water to cover the lamb. Bring to a boil, lower the heat, and simmer, skimming the fat from the stew as it cooks, for about 8 minutes, or long enough to remove some of the impurities.

3. Add the tomatoes, onions, herb bouquet, toasted spices, ginger, garlic, saffron, and a pinch of salt. Cover the pan partway and simmer for 35 minutes, stirring occasionally; add water if you feel it's getting too dry.

4. Remove the lid and the herb bouquet. Simmer over low heat for 10 minutes, then add the vegetables and/or chickpeas, if using. Cook for another 20 minutes, or until the lamb is fork-tender.

5. Taste the stew and season with salt, pepper, lemon, and agave.

poached chicken with crushed potatoes

{ Serves 2 to 4 }

I love poaching food, like this chicken, because poaching couldn't be simpler and it produces the most tender, flavorful meat. Use the poaching liquid left over in the bag as your sauce—it's the best bit. I serve this chicken on Crushed Potatoes with Asparagus and Tomato. It's such a quick dinner, but so satisfying.

Equipment: kitchen twine

4 boneless, skinless organic, free-range chicken thighs, cut into thirds

A few fresh thyme sprigs

2 fresh rosemary sprigs

1 or 2 unpeeled garlic cloves, crushed

Zest of ½ lemon (optional)

2 tablespoons extra virgin olive oil

Maldon or other flaky salt

Freshly ground black pepper

⅔ cup sauvignon blanc or other white wine

Crushed Potatoes with Asparagus and Tomato (page 240), optional

1 small handful fresh parsley leaves, for garnish

1. Preheat the oven to 400°F.

2. In a large bowl, combine the chicken, thyme, rosemary, garlic, lemon zest, and olive oil. Season with salt and pepper.

3. Set out 2 medium bowls and place a large piece of wax paper over each bowl to make a well. Split the chicken mixture evenly between the 2 bowls, bringing the sides of the wax paper up around the

chicken. Pour ⅓ cup of the wine into each paper parcel and tie each one with twine (as shown in the pictures).

4. Place the parcels on a baking sheet and bake for 20 minutes, or until the chicken is cooked through.

5. To serve, either place the little parcels on the table and let guests rip them open themselves, or serve the chicken plated over the Crushed Potatoes with Asparagus and Tomato. Be sure to spoon the wonderful juices on top—they're the best part! Finish with a sprinkle of parsley.

polenta meatballs with quick red wine and tomato sauce

{ Serves 6 }

I love meatballs! I actually don't know anyone who doesn't (who isn't a vegetarian). They're wholesome and comforting.

I've used cornmeal instead of bread crumbs to make these gluten-free, and a touch healthier too. The addition of the lemon, herbs, and fennel seeds also makes them a little more ballsy. Sorry—it's true, though!

red wine and tomato sauce

Two 15-ounce cans diced tomatoes

1¾ cups red wine (such as merlot)

3 fresh thyme sprigs

1 squeeze agave nectar

3 fresh basil leaves

1 garlic clove, thinly sliced

Maldon or other flaky salt

Freshly ground black pepper

meatballs

⅓ cup pine nuts

½ pound good-quality organic ground pork

½ pound good-quality organic ground beef

¼ red onion, finely chopped

2 garlic cloves, minced

2 tablespoons fennel seeds, pounded in a mortar and pestle or chopped

2 tablespoons fresh thyme leaves, chopped

1 large handful fresh flat-leaf parsley, chopped

Zest of 1 lemon

Maldon or other flaky salt

Freshly ground black pepper

2 egg yolks

¼ cup cornmeal

Extra virgin olive oil

Cooked pasta of your choice, for serving

Grated Parmesan cheese, for garnish

Fresh basil and parsley leaves, for garnish

1. To make the tomato sauce, place the tomatoes in a saucepan, then pour the wine into the empty can and add it to the saucepan as well. Add the thyme, agave nectar, basil, and garlic; season with salt and pepper, give it a good stir, and bring to a light simmer over medium-low heat. Keep an eye on it so that it doesn't boil or get too dry, stirring every so often, for about 30 minutes, until the tomatoes have started to break up and it has a sauce consistency.

2. To make the meatballs, in a small dry skillet over medium-low heat, toast the pine nuts until evenly browned, 2 to 3 minutes, stirring often so that they don't burn. Transfer them to a mortar and pestle and grind them until slightly crushed (or simply chop them).

3. In a large bowl, combine the pine nuts, pork, beef, onion, garlic, fennel, thyme, parsley, lemon zest, and salt and pepper to taste and mix thoroughly with your hands. This is a time when your hands will do a far better job than any utensil or machine. When the mixture is well combined, add the egg yolks and cornmeal and mix again.

4. Give the meat a little taste. (Don't worry that it's not cooked—I taste things before I cook all the time, and I'm probably the healthiest person I know.) It's vitally important that the meatballs are seasoned well; if not, you might as well be making any old meatball. Adjust the seasonings as desired.

5. Refrigerate the meat mixture for 10 to 20 minutes to let the meat rest and the flavors mingle.

6. Form the meat into any size meatballs you like. I like mine a little smaller than golf balls.

7. Get a skillet super-hot and add a lug of olive oil. When the oil starts smoking, add the meatballs (you may need to work in batches, depending on the size of your pan) and cook them on all sides

until browned, about 3 minutes total. Turn the heat off, put all the meatballs back into the skillet, add the tomato sauce, and cook for another 3 minutes or so.

8. When you're ready to serve, pour the meatballs and sauce over freshly cooked pasta and top with some grated Parmesan cheese. Scatter a few fresh basil leaves on top.

roast leg of lamb

{ Serves 6 to 8 }

This is a very simple recipe to make an already great-tasting piece of meat even better, and it's a very versatile dish—you could go hot and serve it traditionally, with potatoes and roast vegetables, such as North African Salad (page 91), along with some toasted pita bread.

A few fresh thyme sprigs	Maldon or other flaky salt
2 fresh rosemary sprigs	Freshly ground black pepper
1 fresh sage sprig	¼ cup extra virgin olive oil
4 garlic cloves, sliced	One 3½-pound leg of lamb
Zest of 1 lemon	

1. Put the thyme, rosemary, sage, garlic, lemon zest, and salt and pepper to taste in a mortar and pestle and roughly smash it all up. It doesn't have to be a paste, but you're releasing all the wonderful oils in the zest and herbs. Add the olive oil and give it a good mix. Let it sit for a few minutes for the flavors to develop. If you don't have a mortar and pestle, just give everything a rough chop on a cutting board.

2. In the meantime, place the lamb in a baking dish. Using a paring knife, make 10 to 15 small holes on each side of the leg.

3. Rub the herb mixture all over the lamb, taking care to use your fingers to push the herbs and garlic into the little holes. This will flavor the whole lamb, not just the outside.

4. Cover the lamb and place it in the refrigerator. Let it sit for up to 24 hours, if you can. It makes a huge difference and the lamb will be very aromatic. It's a beautiful thing. If you don't have the time for a

full 24 hours, no problem at all, but do give it a couple of hours to come to room temperature before you put it in the oven.

5. When you're near ready to roast the lamb, preheat the oven to 400°F. Roast the lamb for 30 minutes, then lower the oven temperature to 350°F and roast for another 50 to 60 minutes, depending on how you like your lamb done. I like mine cooked until the inside temperature is at 140°F to 150°F—check it with a meat thermometer.

6. Cover the lamb with foil and set aside to rest for 15 minutes. This resting is a really important step to prevent the juices from rushing out of the meat. If you leave it to rest, all those beautiful juices will distribute back into the meat and create the juiciest possible piece of lamb.

On the baking tray, ready to go.

thai curry

{ Serves 4 to 6 }

A lovely bowl of Thai curry served with lime and cilantro rice is a favorite with guests on the boat, and serving this dish is a surefire way to get on the good side of my crewmates. I like to serve it with an Asian slaw on the side, and, if you can find them, shrimp crackers are a treat too.

You can make the curry as hot or mild as you like. I prefer it hot, but I know some people are sensitive . . . every New Zealand crewmate I've ever worked with has a surprisingly low tolerance to heat, so if you're feeding Kiwis, keep it mild!

1 tablespoon coriander seeds

2 teaspoons cumin seeds

½ teaspoon black peppercorns

2 thumb-size pieces ginger, grated

3 garlic cloves, thinly sliced

1 green or red serrano chile, sliced,
   including seeds

¼ cup chopped fresh cilantro stems

2 lemongrass stalks, tender parts
   roughly chopped

2 tablespoons vegetable oil

½ red onion, finely chopped

Two 14-ounce cans coconut milk

1½ tablespoons fish sauce

1 medium eggplant, cut into 1-inch cubes

1 zucchini, cut into 1-inch pieces

6 organic, free-range chicken thighs,
   each cut into 6 pieces

Juice of 1 to 2 limes

1 tablespoon sugar

1 large handful fresh cilantro leaves,
   roughly chopped

1 handful fresh mint leaves, roughly
   chopped

1 handful fresh basil leaves, roughly
   chopped

Maldon or other flaky salt

Lime and Cilantro Rice (page 250)

Optional garnishes: lime wedges, sliced
   chiles, fresh cilantro sprigs

1. To make the curry paste, smash the coriander, cumin, and
   peppercorns in a mortar and pestle. Don't be afraid to make noise.
   Really smash and pound them until they become a powder, then add
   the ginger, garlic, chile, cilantro stems, and lemongrass and pound
   again. This will take a few minutes of stress-relieving effort. Stop
   when it looks like a paste and starts smelling beautiful.

2. Heat the vegetable oil in a large saucepan over medium-low heat.
   Add the onion and sweat it down until it's translucent and sweet, 3 to
   4 minutes. Add the curry paste, making sure you scrape everything
   out of the mortar and pestle. Cook for about 5 minutes to release the
   flavors, stirring often and taking care that the mixture doesn't burn.

3. Add the coconut milk and give it a stir. Fill the coconut milk cans with water and add the water to the pan. Add the fish sauce, stir to combine, and simmer for at least 30 minutes, until it's thickened. (Note: From here you could either let it cool down and place it in the fridge until you're ready to use it, or continue to finish the curry.)

4. Add the eggplant and cook for 10 to 15 minutes, until the eggplant has softened. Add the zucchini and chicken and cook for 15 minutes, or until the chicken is tender. (The wonderful thing about chicken thighs is that they don't need to cook for a long time, and when they're just cooked, they're the most juicy, tender piece of meat.)

5. To finish the dish off, season it up with the juice of 1 or 2 limes, depending on how juicy they are, the sugar, herbs, and salt to taste. Check the seasoning. This is a really important step, because it'll bring out all the effort you put into your curry paste.

6. Serve the curry with a bowl of steaming hot Lime and Cilantro Rice. You could also garnish it with some lime wedges, sliced chiles, and cilantro sprigs.

NOTE: *This Thai curry doesn't have to be made with chicken. You can drop some shrimp in at the last minute and make it a seafood curry, or just add vegetables and tofu. The most important thing here is really the paste, and to make the most of it, finish the curry well: lots of lime, enough sweetness to balance that, salt, and plenty of fresh herbs.*

whole stuffed chicken

{ Serves 4 }

This is one tasty chicken. The spaghettini might seem like a funny addition, but it soaks up and cooks in the juices of the chicken, mushrooms, and tomatoes so it ends up with the most wonderful texture. I was at a meat counter in San Francisco ordering a deboned chicken when the woman next to me asked what I'd be doing with it. Instead of telling her I'd be stuffing it with mushrooms and prosciutto, I just said, "Pasta." I'm not sure where it came from, but I felt obligated to try it!

This recipe might be off-putting because of all the instructions, but it's just so you understand the process the first time. After that, it's easy. The tying up may seem a little awkward at first, but once you've made this a couple of times, the whole process will take about 15 minutes (and you'll look like a pro).

This is a great dish for entertaining. You can stuff the chicken in advance and keep it wrapped up in the fridge.

Equipment: 10 pieces of kitchen twine, each cut to 12 to 15 inches

Extra virgin olive oil

½ red onion, finely chopped

2 garlic cloves, minced

5 to 6 ounces oyster mushrooms, diced

2 tablespoons finely chopped fresh thyme

1½ tomatoes, diced

⅓ cup sauvignon blanc or other white wine

1 handful fresh flat-leaf parsley, roughly chopped

4 ounces soft goat cheese

Maldon or other flaky salt

Freshly ground black pepper

One 2½- to 3-pound organic, free-range chicken, deboned

2 ounces uncooked spaghettini

3 ounces prosciutto

2 handfuls spinach leaves, optional

1 cup sauvignon blanc or other white wine or water

1. Preheat the oven to 400°F.

2. Heat a few lugs of olive oil in a skillet over low heat. Add the onion and garlic and sweat for 3 to 4 minutes.

3. Add the mushrooms and thyme and another lug of olive oil if you feel it's too dry. Cook for 4 minutes or so, then add the tomatoes and cook for another 2 minutes. Add the wine and let it simmer away and reduce until the moisture has almost (but not completely) evaporated. Gently mix in the parsley and big dollops of goat cheese. Season really well with salt and pepper. This is important, as it'll act as seasoning for the chicken too.

4. Lay the chicken out flat, skin side down, on a clean surface. I like to work on some wax paper—it's easier to clean up, and it'll catch any juices that you can then pour into the baking dish. With a sharp

knife, make some slits lengthwise in the breasts on the back side, not the skin side. They are the thickest part of the chicken and you want to be able to push as much of the stuffing down into them as you can.

5. Spoon the mushroom mixture inside the chicken, using your hands to really get in there. Shove the stuffing in the legs, in the slits you made in the breasts, and so forth. Crack the spaghettini into rough pieces (it's a rustic dish) and shove them in too. They'll soak up the juices from the chicken and the stuffing and will be amazing. Don't worry too much about overstuffing; if you put too much stuffing in, it'll just kind of squish out when you tie it up. Lay the prosciutto over the top of the stuffing (see photo, page 215).

6. To tie up the chicken, fold the legs back over and place a piece of string under the chicken. Slowly pull the ends together and make a little knot. Don't pull too tight—if you squeeze it too tight now, it'll push the insides out. Continue tying the chicken with the rest of the string until it's nicely secure and relatively tight.

7. Place the chicken breast side down in a baking dish. I throw some spinach leaves in the dish first because it makes a nice bed, and the spinach cooks deliciously in the chicken juices, but it's totally optional. Add any leftover stuffing to the bottom of the baking dish and pour any leftover juices over the chicken. This is the stuff flavor comes from.

8. Season the outside of the chicken very well with salt and pepper, along with a generous drizzle of olive oil. Pour the wine or water (or a mixture of both) into the baking dish and place in the oven.

9. Roast the chicken for about 1 hour or less, depending on the size of the bird. Check it every now and then to see how it's going, and take

the opportunity to baste the chicken when you do. I'm a big-time baster—just use a spoon to pour the cooking juices back over the top. The best way to test that the chicken is done is to check the internal temperature; it shouldn't go over 165°F. I usually like to go to 160°F, because the chicken will continue cooking after it's removed from the oven.

10. Cover the chicken with foil and let it rest for at least 15 minutes. Don't be tempted to dive straight in, because it'll just lose all the incredible juices. If you let it sit, the juices will settle gently into everything.

11. To serve, carefully remove the strings and cut the chicken into ½-inch-thick slices, or your desired thickness. Serve with some crusty fresh bread and a leafy green salad with a lemony vinaigrette.

NOTE: *I can't say it enough: Improvise. Throw some spinach into the stuffing or some pine nuts. And you don't have to use pasta—you could stuff the chicken with couscous, quinoa, anything you like. Have fun!*

roast chicken stuffed with fennel, potatoes, bacon, and apricots

{ Serves 4 to 6 }

Sometimes people want the comforts of old classics, but also want to feel like they're having something a bit different. This is the dish for such an occasion. It's basically two dishes in one: a veg/side and a roast chicken, except that you're cooking the side dish inside the chicken to give it a lot of extra flavor. In fact, it's kind of like a stuffing, but without the eggs and bread. And it dirties only two cooking vessels, which is always a bonus for a full meal.

One 4-pound organic, free-range chicken

½ cup pine nuts

4 strips uncured organic bacon, roughly chopped

½ large fennel bulb, thinly sliced

1 leek, white part only, thinly sliced

1 russet potato (about 7 ounces), scrubbed and cut into ½-inch pieces

2 fresh thyme sprigs

1 fresh oregano sprig

2 garlic cloves, minced

1 teaspoon fennel seeds, crushed

Maldon or other flaky salt

Extra virgin olive oil

1½ cups ale (I use Newcastle Brown Ale)

1 bay leaf

9 apricots, thinly sliced

Freshly ground black pepper

1 handful fresh flat-leaf parsley leaves, roughly chopped

Zest of 1 lemon

2 tablespoons unsalted butter

1. Set the oven rack to the lower third of the oven and preheat the oven to 450°F. Remove the chicken from the fridge to lose its chill.

2. Toast the pine nuts as directed on page 14. Transfer to a small bowl and set aside.

3. Increase the heat under the skillet to medium, add the bacon, and cook until crispy, 4 to 5 minutes. Reduce the heat to medium-low and add the fennel, leek, potato, thyme, oregano, garlic, and fennel seeds, along with a pinch of salt. You could also add a tablespoon of olive oil if it looks too dry. Cook for about 10 minutes, until the vegetables have softened and caramelized slightly.

4. Add ¾ cup of the ale, the bay leaf, apricots, and pine nuts, and cook for another few minutes, until the liquid has almost evaporated.

5. Check the seasoning and adjust as desired. Season with black pepper and add the parsley and lemon zest. Let the mixture cool for a few minutes.

6. Stuff the cavity of the chicken with the vegetable mixture. If any doesn't fit, just place it in the roasting pan as a bed for the chicken.

7. Slice the butter and place it under the chicken skin over the breasts. Rub about a tablespoon of olive oil over the whole chicken and season generously with salt and pepper. Set the chicken in the roasting pan and add the remaining ¾ cup ale to the pan.

8. Turn the oven temperature down to 400°F and place the roasting pan in the oven. Roast for 1 hour and 15 minutes to 1 hour and 30 minutes, depending on your oven. After an hour, check the internal temperature of the chicken; it shouldn't go above 165°F. The skin will be a rich, dark golden brown color, but don't go by that alone. If you're in doubt, cut into it—just make sure you don't overcook it. No one likes a dry chicken.

9. Let the chicken rest under aluminum foil for about 15 minutes before carving and serving with the vegetables.

lamb and quinoa koftas on soft chickpeas with toasted pita bread

{ Serves 2 to 3 }

It's amazing how much flavor you can shove into one little ball. Here's another version of a nontraditional kofta. Serve this with the Haydari (Turkish dipping sauce; page 278).

lamb

¼ cup uncooked quinoa

½ pound best-quality ground lamb

2 tablespoons minced red onion

1 large garlic clove, minced

1 teaspoon ground cumin

1 teaspoon ground coriander

¼ teaspoon ground sumac

Pinch cayenne pepper

Leaves from ⅓ bunch fresh cilantro, minced

Zest of ½ lemon

Maldon or other flaky salt

Freshly ground black pepper

chickpeas

1 teaspoon ground cumin

2 tablespoons olive oil

½ red onion, finely chopped

1 large garlic clove, minced

One 15-ounce can chickpeas

Maldon or other flaky salt

Freshly ground black pepper

½ lemon

3 tablespoons extra virgin olive oil

2 large pieces pita bread, cut into 1½-inch strips

1 handful fresh cilantro leaves, for garnish

1. Cook the quinoa according to the package directions and drain. Place back over the heat and stir for a minute to remove any excess moisture. Remove from the heat and cool.

2. In a large bowl, combine the lamb, onion, garlic, cumin, coriander, sumac, cayenne, cilantro, and lemon zest; season with salt and pepper. Give it a good mix with your hands, add the quinoa, and mix again until the ingredients are evenly distributed. I taste mine here and encourage you to do the same.

3. Cover the lamb mixture in plastic wrap and refrigerate it for at least 30 minutes, or up to 6 hours, to firm up a little.

4. Meanwhile, prepare the chickpeas. Add the cumin to a dry sauté pan and toast it for a couple of minutes over low heat, stirring often, until fragrant. Add the olive oil to the pan, then the onion and garlic, and sweat them down for about 5 minutes, still over low heat (you're not looking for them to brown). Add the chickpeas along with the liquid

in the can. Season with a little salt and pepper and simmer for about 10 minutes. You want the chickpeas to be fork tender but not so soft that they don't hold together. Give the pan a shake every now and then.

5. Remove the pan from the heat and let the chickpeas cool a bit. Add a squeeze of lemon juice and check the seasoning. (You'll be reheating the chickpeas quickly when the koftas are cooked.)

6. Remove the lamb mixture from the fridge and form it into football shapes. I start by rolling meatballs the size of a golf ball and then I squash them a little to elongate them. Or you can make the meatballs in any shape you like.

7. When you're ready to eat, heat a large sauté pan over medium-high heat and add a couple of tablespoons of olive oil. Get the pan pretty hot, but not smoking hot. You want to get nice color on the lamb, but not so much heat that the outsides burn before the insides cook. Place the meatballs one by one in the pan and cook them for about 4 minutes each, until browned on the outside and cooked through in the middle. (If you want to prepare them in advance, cook them for a couple of minutes in a very hot pan to give them some color and then transfer them to a baking dish. When you're ready to serve, finish them off in a 400°F oven for a few minutes.)

8. While the meatballs are cooking, gently warm the chickpeas over low heat.

9. Place the warmed chickpeas on a serving platter and top with the meatballs. Keep the heat going on the sauté pan that held the meatballs and use that oil to fry the pita bread strips, about 1 minute on each side. Place the pita strips on the side of the platter, top the whole thing with cilantro leaves, and serve.

Top left:
Costa Rica.

*Right and
bottom left:*
Solomon Islands.

Sides

baked lima beans

{ Serves 6 }

I know I've said it before, but I'm such a big fan of beans. In the winter I love to prepare them this way with a roast chicken. They're good comfort food.

2 tablespoons extra virgin olive oil	Zest of 1 lemon
¼ red onion, finely chopped	Maldon or other flaky salt
3 garlic cloves, minced	Freshly ground black pepper
Leaves from 2 fresh thyme sprigs	Agave nectar
Four 15-ounce cans lima beans, drained	1 bay leaf
Two 15-ounce cans diced tomatoes	1 handful feta cheese, optional
2 teaspoons powdered mustard	

1. Preheat the oven to 275°F.

2. Heat the olive oil in a medium saucepan over low heat, add the onion, garlic, and thyme, and sweat until the onion is softened, 4 to 5 minutes.

3. Add the beans and cook them lightly for a few minutes, then add the tomatoes, mustard, lemon zest, a couple of good pinches of salt, pepper to taste, a good squeeze of agave, and the bay leaf. Bring to a mild simmer and cook for 15 minutes, stirring occasionally.

4. Check the seasoning, pour the mixture into a 2-quart baking dish, and cover it with foil. Be sure to use a large enough baking dish, or the mixture will bubble over and make a mess. Bake the beans for 30 minutes, or until they are soft and have soaked up the liquid in the

baking dish, and it looks as though everything is melded together. If you like, for the last 5 minutes of cooking, remove the foil, add some feta, and give it a little mix through. Serve hot.

bean casserole

{ Serves 4 }

Beans are so good at soaking up flavor, and they go with almost anything. I like serving bean casseroles to the crew—the boys are always on massive protein kicks, so beans are quite popular. I also recently started adding ginger to beans—what a match! This is great with roast chicken and an arugula salad.

Extra virgin olive oil

¼ red onion, finely chopped

1 large thumb-size piece ginger, minced

2 garlic cloves, minced

Three 15-ounce cans beans, drained (I recommend 1 cannellini, 1 pinto, and 1 red kidney)

Leaves from 7 fresh thyme sprigs

¼ cup apple cider vinegar

2 tablespoons good-quality ketchup

1 tablespoon Dijon mustard

Maldon or other flaky salt

Freshly ground black pepper

1. Preheat the oven to 300°F.

2. Heat a little olive oil in a large saucepan over low heat. Add the onion, ginger, and garlic and sweat for about 4 minutes to get the onion translucent and sweet, which is what you're looking for.

3. Add the beans, thyme, vinegar, ketchup, and mustard. Cook for another 2 minutes or so, until the mixture comes together. Season with salt and pepper and taste to check the seasoning.

4. Pour the mixture into a baking dish, cover it with foil, and punch a few small holes in the foil. (Be sure to use a large enough baking dish, or the mixture will bubble over and make a mess.) Bake for 1 hour, or until the beans are soft, have soaked up the liquid, and have melded together.

5. Let the casserole sit for a couple of minutes to cool, then serve.

beer tempura with simple dipping sauce

{ Serves 2 }

This is an easy alternative way to make tempura, and the results are wonderfully crisp. The beer gives the tempura mixture a great depth, and the cilantro and sesame seeds are interesting additions to the batter.

The recipe makes about 3 cups of batter, but what you fry depends on you. I've given a few examples of foods to use, but try what you like.

simple dipping sauce

½ cup soy sauce

¼ cup rice vinegar

1 tablespoon minced fresh ginger

1 teaspoon agave nectar

1 small handful fresh cilantro leaves, finely chopped

A few fresh basil leaves, finely chopped

2 teaspoons red chile flakes

tempura

1 cup all-purpose flour

Maldon or other flaky salt

1 tablespoon cornstarch

1½ cups ice-cold beer (I use Sapporo, but you can use whatever you have in your fridge)

2 tablespoons sesame seeds, optional

2 tablespoons finely chopped fresh cilantro stalks, optional

Vegetable oil, for frying

Foods to fry, such as shrimp, sugar snap peas, bok choy, eggplant—the possibilities are endless!

1. To make the dipping sauce, combine all the ingredients in a nonreactive bowl.

2. To make the batter, combine the flour, salt, and cornstarch in a large bowl and slowly whisk in the beer until smooth. If you're going to add the sesame seeds and/or cilantro, do it now.

3. Place a saucepan filled with about 5 inches of oil over high heat and bring to about 350°F. This doesn't actually take very long, and you don't need a thermometer to know when it's ready—just throw in a little piece of vegetable or batter, and if the oil starts bubbling straightaway, it's ready.

4. When you're ready to start frying, place the pieces of food in the batter one by one to coat and then gently place them away from you into the hot oil. You can fry a few pieces at a time, depending on the size of your pan. Leave them in the oil for 2 to 3 minutes, until they're a nice golden color.

5. Remove the tempura-battered items one by one with a slotted spoon and place them on a plate lined with a paper towel to soak up the oil. Serve as soon as possible with the dipping sauce.

brussels sprouts and oyster mushrooms with pine nuts

{ Serves 4 }

If you're not keen on Brussels sprouts, pretend you've forgotten and make this recipe anyway. I'm not their biggest fan, but I could eat a whole bowl of this. Try it.

¼ cup pine nuts

Extra virgin olive oil

3 strips bacon, diced

8 ounces oyster mushrooms, roughly torn

Hazelnut oil

10 Brussels sprouts, trimmed, halved, and thinly sliced

¼ red onion, minced

1 tablespoon balsamic vinegar

Freshly ground black pepper

Maldon or other flaky salt

Agave nectar

1. In a small dry skillet over low heat, toast the pine nuts until golden, 3 to 4 minutes, stirring often.

2. Get a sauté pan smoking hot and add a tiny bit of olive oil and the bacon. Cook until the bacon is nice and crispy, but don't let it burn— you just want to cook the fat off and brown it a bit, about 2 minutes. Add the mushrooms and sauté until they have some color and have soaked up all the rendered bacon fat in the pan, about 4 minutes.

3. Pour a small lug of hazelnut oil into the pan. Add the Brussels sprouts and onion to the mixture and toss around for 30 seconds to 1 minute.

You want to keep the green color and make sure they don't get too wilted.

4. To finish it off, add the vinegar, a few good twists of pepper, salt, and a touch of agave nectar. Add the pine nuts, toss around again a few times, and serve.

chickpea and corn falafel

{ Serves 4 to 6 }

This takes a bit more effort than most of my recipes, but it's such a great little dish. You'll feel really satisfied when it's done, especially if you make it for friends. Serve it as an appetizer with some toasted pita bread and Haydari sauce or Hummus, or as part of a meal with a lovely piece of roast lamb, some pita bread, dips, and a leafy salad.

2 tablespoons extra virgin olive oil	1 bay leaf
¼ red onion, minced	Freshly ground black pepper
1 large or 2 small garlic cloves, minced	1 cup yellow cornmeal
1 tablespoon ground cumin	1 lemon
1 tablespoon ground allspice	About 1 quart vegetable oil, for frying
One 15-ounce can chickpeas	All-purpose flour, for dusting
Maldon or other flaky salt	Haydari (page 278) or Hummus (page 283), optional
2 cups whole milk	

1. Heat the olive oil in a large saucepan over low heat. Add the onion and garlic and sweat for 3 to 4 minutes, until the onion is translucent and soft.

2. Add the cumin and allspice and cook, stirring, for 1 to 2 minutes, to toast the spices and bring out their flavor. Just don't let them burn!

3. Add the chickpeas along with their liquid and a good pinch of salt. Turn the heat up and simmer, stirring occasionally to make sure nothing is sticking or burning. After about 6 minutes, the chickpeas

should be fork tender. Use the back of a fork to lightly crush them, but keep some texture—you're not looking to make a puree.

4. Add the milk and give it a good stir. Add the bay leaf and a pinch of salt and slowly bring to a simmer again. Cook the mixture down for another 7 minutes or so, stirring occasionally and monitoring the heat. Don't let it cook too quickly, or it'll catch the bottom of the pan and burn.

5. Remove the bay leaf and reduce the heat to low. Add the cornmeal and stir with a wooden spoon to incorporate. Take care—it's a hot mixture and it might spit like a little volcano. If this happens, just take it off the heat and keep stirring. Cook for 7 to 8 minutes, until the cornmeal is mostly cooked through but still a bit grainy—give it a taste to check.

6. Mix in some black pepper, more salt, and a squeeze of lemon. You almost want to overseason the mixture a bit, because by the time it's rested in the fridge and cooked again, the seasoning will have become a bit muted.

7. Remove the mixture from the pan and flatten it onto a plate. Cover with plastic wrap and place in the fridge to cool down for at least 30 minutes. (You can prepare the recipe up to this stage 1 or 2 days in advance.)

8. When you're ready to eat, pour the vegetable oil into a large saucepan and heat it over medium-high heat.

9. While you're waiting for your oil to heat up, form the falafel. Roll the mixture in your hands to make balls about the size of a golf ball, then gently press them with your palms to form a football shape. The shape isn't too important, but I do find this shape is easiest to

work with and creates great crunchy ends and a soft middle. Place the falafels in a small tray of flour and roll them to coat lightly.

10. To test the oil, place a pea-size piece of the mixture into the pot—when it rises to the surface and starts bubbling, turning a deep gold color, you're ready to cook. Place one falafel into the oil and fry for 4 to 5 minutes, until it's a deep golden color—I like to test one after cooking to make sure it's piping hot all the way through. Serve warm.

crushed potatoes with asparagus and tomato

{ Serves 2 to 4 }

I've paired this dish with Poached Chicken, but it would also be lovely with a piece of poached fish. It's a wonderfully tasty dish, and *so* quick. You just put everything in a pot, smash it up, season, and it's done!

1 pound baby potatoes, halved (I like to use the different colors)

About 12 spears of asparagus, cut into 1-inch pieces

4 ounces cherry tomatoes, halved

¼ cup extra virgin olive oil

Zest of ½ lemon

Maldon or other flaky salt

Freshly ground black pepper

1 handful fresh dill, chopped (no big stems)

1 handful fresh flat-leaf parsley, chopped

Poached Chicken (page 197), optional, for serving

1. Bring a pot of salted water to a boil. Add the potatoes and cook for 15 minutes, or until they're just about to fall apart. They should crush easily when pressed with the back of a fork but not be so soft that they're ready to mash.

2. When your potatoes are about ready, add the asparagus and cherry tomatoes and let them finish cooking with the potatoes. Drain when the asparagus is crisp-tender. Let sit for a couple of minutes so that the vegetables steam off some excess water.

3. Place the potatoes, asparagus, and tomatoes in a large bowl and add the olive oil and lemon zest; season with salt and pepper. Give it a good mix around—the potatoes will soak up the olive oil and the

beautiful lemon zest flavor while they're warm. If the potatoes aren't slightly breaking up on their own, pinch them a bit with your fingers to help them along.

4. When you're ready to serve, season well and add the fresh herbs. Serve underneath Poached Chicken, if you like, with the beautiful juices from the chicken drizzled over the crushed potatoes.

cumin pita bread/plain pita bread with spiced oil

{ Makes about 10 pitas }

This is a really simple pita bread recipe, and it's so satisfying to make yourself, either in the oven or as a flatbread on top of the stove (see Note). One of my sous-chefs, DeWaal van Heerden, used to make a flatbread with cumin seeds, and it's a great idea. Now I add cumin to my pitas when I'm serving them with a Middle Eastern–style lunch.

pita dough

1 package (¼ ounce) active dry yeast

½ cup warm water

2 teaspoons agave nectar or 1 teaspoon sugar

3 cups all-purpose flour

1½ teaspoons salt

2½ teaspoons ground cumin, optional

1 teaspoon cumin seeds, optional

1 cup lukewarm water

Extra virgin olive oil

spiced oil

2 fresh oregano sprigs

1 garlic clove

Pinch Maldon or other flaky salt

2 tablespoons extra virgin olive oil

1. In a small bowl, combine the yeast, warm water, and agave nectar and let it sit in a warm place for about 15 minutes. You'll see that the yeast is starting to work when it bubbles.

2. In the meantime, combine the flour, salt, and cumin, if desired, in a large bowl. Make a little well in the center and lightly flour the work surface.

3. Add the yeast mixture to the flour mixture and incorporate with one hand. Add the lukewarm water and slowly incorporate it. Bring it all together to form a lump of dough, turn it onto the floured surface, and knead it with both hands for a solid 10 minutes, or until smooth and elastic. If you feel you're not quite there yet, give it another couple of minutes of kneading.

4. Place the dough in a large bowl, lightly rub the dough with some oil, and set it in a warm place to rise for 2 to 3 hours, until at least doubled in size.

5. Meanwhile, to make the spiced oil, combine the oregano, garlic, and salt in a mortar and pestle and smash it up. Mix in the olive oil and let it sit for at least 1 hour before using.

6. Place a baking sheet in the oven and preheat it to 500°F, or the hottest setting you have.

7. For each piece of pita bread, roll a bit of dough into a ball just a little bigger than a golf ball (you'll get about 10 pitas out of the dough). Use a rolling pin to roll each ball into a circle that's about ¼ inch thick and about 5 to 6 inches across.

8. Bake each piece of pita on the hot baking sheet, about 2½ minutes on each side, until it's puffed up and has some good color on it. I make 3 or 4 at a time. Brush the spiced oil over the warm baked pita.

NOTE: *To cook as flatbread, get a dry skillet really hot and cook the rolled-out pita dough one at a time for 2 to 3 minutes on each side.*

stuffed pita breads

{ Makes 10 pita pockets }

These are the greatest! A cook I know from El Salvador told me about pupusas, which are basically stuffed corn tortilla breads. It's such a cool idea, and I thought it might work well with pita bread dough as well—and it does. They're so tasty, and this is a fun way to use up leftovers—you can make these with any leftover meat, such as lamb, chicken, or beef, and top with some fresh arugula and cheese. The recipe below is only a suggestion—stuff them with anything you like. Definitely a crowd pleaser.

2 handfuls arugula

2 tomatoes

4 ounces fresh mozzarella cheese

⅛ red onion, minced

1 garlic clove, minced

Extra virgin olive oil

Maldon or other flaky salt

Freshly ground black pepper

1 recipe Plain Pita Bread (page 243), prepared through step 7 (minus the spice oil), or store-bought pizza dough

1. Place the arugula, tomatoes, mozzarella, and onion on a cutting board and finely chop all together. Place in a bowl with the garlic and mix. Drizzle with a tablespoon of olive oil and season well with salt and pepper.

2. Dust your left hand (if you're a righty) with some flour and place a dough circle flat in the palm of that hand. With your other (dominant) hand, take a small handful of the salad mixture and squeeze it, making it small enough to place in your palm, as if the dough circle were a baseball glove. Bring the dough together at the top to wrap

around the salad mixture and seal with your fingertips. Carefully flatten the ball between the palms of your hands to make a disk about ½ inch thick. Repeat with the remaining dough circles and salad mixture (see photos).

3. Place each stuffed pita in a very hot, dry sauté pan and cook for about 2 minutes on each side, until golden, and serve.

lime and cilantro rice

{ Serves 4 }

This is the first rice recipe I ever made in culinary school. I'd really never even made rice before! Years later, I'm still making it.

2 cups uncooked jasmine rice

2 handfuls fresh cilantro leaves, roughly chopped

1 handful fresh mint leaves, roughly torn

Juice of 2 limes

1 tablespoon vegetable oil

1 teaspoon sesame oil, optional

Maldon or other flaky salt

Freshly ground black pepper

1. Rinse the rice under cold running water until the water runs clear.

2. Cook the rice according to the package instructions.

3. Add the cilantro, mint, lime juice, vegetable oil, and, if you like, sesame oil. Season well with salt and pepper and serve hot.

mushroom, pea, and corn ragout

{ Serves 2 to 4 }

I used to make this ragout when I lived and worked at a vineyard in the Napa Valley. Chanterelle mushrooms are easily found there, and you should use them if possible—they're the best. This is lovely with some spring lamb.

2 ears fresh corn

Extra virgin olive oil

Maldon or other flaky salt

Freshly ground black pepper

1 cup oyster mushrooms, roughly chopped or torn

¼ red onion, finely chopped

2 garlic cloves, minced

2 fresh thyme sprigs

About 10 asparagus spears, cut into 1-inch-long pieces

¾ cup cooked lima beans

¾ cup green peas, preferably fresh

¼ pound green beans, halved

½ cup shelled fava beans

Zest of ½ lemon

1 handful fresh flat-leaf parsley leaves, roughly chopped

1. Preheat the oven to 500°F.

2. Cover a baking sheet with aluminum foil, place the corn on it, cover with a good lug of olive oil, and sprinkle with salt and pepper. Roast the corn for about 10 minutes, until it is nicely colored. Cool slightly, then use a paring knife to remove the kernels from the cobs. Set aside.

3. Get a sauté pan smoking hot over high heat and add a tablespoon or so of olive oil, the mushrooms, and some salt and pepper. Toss them around until they have some good color on them, about 4 minutes.

4. In a large saucepan, heat 2 tablespoons olive oil over low heat, add the onion, garlic, and thyme, and sweat until the onion is softened, 4 to 5 minutes. Add the asparagus, lima beans, peas, green beans, fava beans, mushrooms, and corn kernels.

5. Increase the heat to medium-high, add a splash of water, cover, and cook for about 3 minutes, so that the vegetables cook quickly and retain their bright green color. Add the lemon zest and season with salt and pepper. Top with the fresh parsley and serve.

moroccan steamed couscous

{ Makes about 4 cups }

My Moroccan friend Naima Benamich, who makes couscous like this, describes a couple of the steps as lightly massaging the couscous. It kind of gets the point across that you're putting a lot of love and effort into the couscous to make it wonderfully light and airy. Serve with Moroccan Lamb (page 195).

2 cups uncooked couscous

1 teaspoon Maldon or other flaky salt

½ teaspoon olive oil

1. Place the couscous in a fine sieve and rinse it under cold water. Spread it out on a baking sheet and let it sit for 5 minutes.

2. Break up the couscous between your fingertips to separate all the grains. Place the couscous back in the sieve and set it over a pot of simmering water. Cover the sieve with aluminum foil and steam the couscous for 15 minutes (see photo).

3. Transfer the couscous to a bowl and work through it again with your fingertips, both aerating it and breaking up any lumps.

4. Transfer it back to the sieve, cover with the foil again, and simmer for another 15 minutes.

5. Return the couscous to the bowl and add the salt and olive oil. Break it up with your fingertips again and serve.

garlic bread stuffed with italian herbs

{ Serves 6 to 8 }

While I was making this recipe to photograph for the book, I was talking about how I'm often too busy to make bread a priority on the boat, but I do bake this bread quite often because it's foolproof and delicious. The photographer's assistant, Janell, was listening when I talked about how to make the bread, and when she went camping that weekend, she made it and cooked it on the fire. What a great idea! It makes me so happy, and if this is something a few friends can enjoy when camping, you know it's a winner!

2 garlic cloves, roughly sliced

⅓ cup loosely packed fresh rosemary leaves, roughly chopped

⅓ cup loosely packed fresh oregano leaves, roughly torn

⅓ cup fresh marjoram leaves, roughly torn

1 small handful fresh flat-leaf parsley leaves, roughly torn

Maldon or other flaky salt

¾ cup extra virgin olive oil

1 loaf of Italian bread (or your favorite unsliced bread)

Freshly ground black pepper

1 handful cherry tomatoes

1 handful black olives

1 handful good-quality feta cheese

1. Preheat the oven to 400°F.

2. Place the garlic, rosemary, oregano, marjoram, parsley, and a good pinch of salt in a mortar and pestle and smash it up for a few minutes. Really go for it! Add the olive oil, give it a good mix around, and set it aside for about 5 minutes to allow the flavors to develop.

3. Cut the bread into vertical slices, but don't cut all the way down to the bottom. You'll be stuffing the slices with deliciousness.

4. Give the herb and garlic mixture another good stir in the mortar and pestle, adjust the seasoning with salt and pepper as desired, and spoon the mixture into the bread between the slices, really filling it up.

5. Give the tomatoes a little squeeze to break them open (watch out for spatters on T-shirts!) and place them inside the bread. Add the olives. Next, crumble the feta into the bread. Drizzle in any olive oil left in the mortar (and add an extra drizzle if you feel the need).

6. Wrap the bread in foil and bake it for 10 minutes. Uncover the top part of the foil to expose the top of the bread and bake for another 7 minutes, or until golden.

7. Serve the bread whole and let people pull off pieces of the bread for themselves.

cardamom rice

{ Serves 4 }

This is my favorite way to cook rice: in a baking dish in the oven. You can add whatever whole spices you want and it'll come out fragrant and wonderful. If you do use whole cardamom, don't eat the pods! You may know that already, but our captain eats them every time and it makes him pull a terrible face.

1 cup uncooked basmati rice	Maldon or other flaky salt
2 or 3 cardamom pods	Freshly ground black pepper
2 tablespoons salted or unsalted butter	½ cup sliced almonds
1 bay leaf	

1. Preheat the oven to 350°F.

2. In an ovenproof dish, combine the rice, cardamom, butter, and bay leaf; season with salt and pepper and add 1 cup water. Cover with foil and bake for about 40 minutes, checking after 35 minutes, depending on your oven. You want the rice to soak up all the water but also to look dry (see photo).

3. In the meantime, toast the almonds in a small dry skillet over medium-low heat until golden brown, stirring often, 3 to 4 minutes. Set aside.

4. Remove the foil and gently fluff the rice with a fork. Check the seasoning, top with the toasted almonds, and serve.

seed loaf

{ Makes one 5-inch × 10-inch loaf }

Baking bread couldn't get any easier than this, really. You basically just throw everything together, mix, and put it in whatever baking vessel you like. My mother has been making this for years. She got the recipe from a friend in our carpool when I was in kindergarten. She makes it in whatever she can find—mostly old coffee tins, which produce a cool, round loaf. She usually makes two at a time—one for everyone else and one for my father, who only likes to eat it after about four days. He slices it really thick, toasts it, puts some butter on it, then eats it with his eyes closed.

2 cups rye flour

2 cups whole wheat flour

1 tablespoon Maldon or other flaky salt

1 package (¼ ounce) instant dry yeast

1¾ cups mixed seeds (I use sesame, flax, poppy, pumpkin, and sunflower)

2 tablespoons extra virgin olive oil

2 tablespoons apple cider vinegar

1 tablespoon agave nectar

1. Preheat the oven to 400°F.

2. Combine the rye and whole wheat flours, salt, yeast, and seeds in a large bowl. Mix in the oil, vinegar, agave nectar, and 2 cups water. It'll all come together in a sticky dough.

3. Place the dough in an oiled loaf pan or tin and press it in. It'll only rise slightly, so you can fill it almost to the top.

4. Bake for about 1 hour. You'll know it's done when it starts to color and pull away from the sides of the pan.

tamarind and coconut lentils

See the photo on page 174 with the Cilantro Fish

{ Serves 4 }

My intention when I made this sauce was to cook and serve it with mussels. DVF told me afterward that she doesn't eat mussels, but she did love the sauce. So the next time I made her this sauce, I made it with lentils instead. It works equally well with both, so if you're looking for a different way to serve mussels, give them a try in this sauce.

1 tablespoon vegetable oil

1 garlic clove, minced

¼ red onion, finely chopped

1 tablespoon minced fresh ginger

½ tablespoon curry powder

1 tablespoon pure tamarind paste (see Note)

One 14-ounce can coconut milk

1½ cups Puy lentils, rinsed

Maldon or other flaky salt

Fish sauce, optional

Agave nectar

1 lime

1 small handful fresh cilantro leaves, chopped

1 small handful fresh basil leaves, chopped

1 small handful fresh mint leaves, chopped

1. Heat the vegetable oil in a medium saucepan over low heat. Add the garlic and onion and sweat for a few minutes, until softened, then add the ginger and curry powder. Stir for another couple of minutes, then add the tamarind paste and cook for another minute or so, until fragrant.

2. Add the coconut milk, keeping the heat low. You don't want the coconut milk to boil, as it will separate. If this happens, whisk vigorously until it comes back together. Simmer lightly for 30 minutes, or until the liquid thickens.

3. In the meantime, cook the lentils in a pot of boiling water for about 20 minutes, until tender, and drain.

4. When the sauce is finished, add the lentils and season with salt, fish sauce, if using, and agave nectar. Finish the sauce with a squeeze of lime juice and the chopped herbs.

NOTE: *You can buy tamarind paste at most supermarkets now. It has a lovely tangy, tart flavor. But store-bought paste often has the seeds and skin in it, which are hard and inedible. You need to soak the paste to remove the unwanted bits. To do this, soak 2 tablespoons store-bought tamarind paste in 3 tablespoons of water for about 5 minutes. After it's soaked, pass it through a sieve to get a smooth paste.*

However, if you are able to purchase tamarind without the seeds, you're good to go as is.

tomato and leek sauce

See the photo on page 155 with the Green Quinoa–Crusted Bass

{ Serves 4 to 6 }

I've served this sauce with so many dishes, such as the Green Quinoa–Crusted Bass. It's really versatile, but also super-easy and low maintenance to cook.

2 tablespoons extra virgin olive oil

2 cups thinly sliced leeks (white and green parts)

2 garlic cloves, minced

2 fresh thyme sprigs

4 tomatoes, roughly chopped

⅓ cup sauvignon blanc or other white wine

Maldon or other flaky salt

Freshly ground black pepper

Agave nectar, optional

1. Heat the olive oil in a medium saucepan over medium-low heat. Add the leeks, garlic, and thyme and sweat until tender but not browned, 8 to 10 minutes, stirring occasionally.

2. Add the tomatoes and wine, season with salt and pepper, and continue to cook for about 30 minutes, until the sauce thickens and everything starts to meld, stirring occasionally.

3. Check the seasoning before serving—it may need a touch of agave nectar.

Temple, Halong Bay,
Vietnam.

Sauces, Dips, and Dressings

arugula and walnut pesto

{ Makes about 1 cup }

There's nothing revolutionary about this pesto, but it's super-tasty and versatile. Use this as an easy pasta sauce or sandwich spread, or try a dollop over a grilled steak.

½ cup walnuts

1 small garlic clove, minced

½ cup extra virgin olive oil

2 handfuls arugula

1 small handful fresh basil leaves

½ cup grated Parmesan cheese

Maldon or other flaky salt

Freshly ground black pepper

1. In a small dry skillet over medium-low heat, toast the walnuts until golden brown, about 3 to 4 minutes, stirring constantly.

2. Combine all the ingredients in a blender and blend until you're happy with the consistency. Some people like their pesto fine and others like a bit of texture to it. I personally like it a bit chunky. Season with more salt and pepper if needed.

eggplant dip

{ Makes about 3 cups }

This is a super-tasty dip that can be used on sandwiches or at a barbecue or picnic. You can also make it with a large zucchini instead of the eggplant—just halve the cooking time.

I've used a mortar and pestle in this recipe—it's one of my favorite tools in the kitchen. It's ideal for something like this because it brings out all of the beautiful oils in the herbs and makes a rough paste of the ingredients. Besides its practical uses, it's also a hugely satisfying tool to use. If you don't have one, no worries—just roughly chop the ingredients together on a cutting board.

1 heaping cup fresh mixed herbs
(rosemary, thyme, oregano, and basil)

½ cup extra virgin olive oil

1 garlic clove, sliced

1 medium to large eggplant

Maldon or other flaky salt

Juice of ½ lemon

Freshly ground black pepper

1. Preheat the oven to 400°F.

2. Put the herbs, garlic, and salt and pepper to taste in a mortar and pestle and grind to work the oil out of the herbs. Do this for a few minutes, then add the olive oil and give a good mix to help the flavors develop.

3. Halve the eggplant lengthwise and crisscross the flesh of the eggplant with a knife (don't cut all the way through).

4. Stuff the herb mixture into the flesh of the eggplant, pushing it in with your fingers until it's really well distributed throughout. Pour any leftover oil on top.

5. Place the eggplant halves back together, wrap the whole eggplant in foil, and roast it for about 45 minutes, until the flesh is soft. To test, just give it a squeeze in the foil—if it feels soft and squishy, it's done.

6. Unwrap the foil (watch out for hot steam!) and scoop out the flesh and herbs (leaving the skin behind). Place it in a food processor and blend until it's almost smooth but still has a little texture. Check the seasoning and add the lemon juice. Serve hot or cold.

avocado and yogurt dipping sauce

{ Makes 1 cup }

I'm trying to think of someone I know who doesn't like avocado . . . and I can't. It's the best. It's so versatile and can add such a wonderful rich creaminess to food that isn't often possible with something that's so good for you. This sauce works really well with Cornmeal Squid (page 146), but you can serve it with anything you like! I also use it as a salad dressing—follow the recipe, then whisk a little bit of water into it at the end.

1 avocado, peeled, pitted, and roughly chopped

2 tablespoons plain yogurt

2 tablespoons fresh lime juice

1 teaspoon minced fresh ginger

2 teaspoons agave nectar

1 tablespoon extra virgin olive oil

Combine all the ingredients in a blender and blend until completely smooth.

haydari

{ Makes 1½ cups}

I spent a bit of time in Turkey last year, and a trip to Istanbul made me fall in love with the food there. The flavors are big and exciting. I make this little dip a lot and serve it with numerous dishes—it's perfect with Lamb and Quinoa Kofta (page 219), but you can also serve it with toasted pita bread or a chopped salad, and it would also be great as a dip with crudités.

6 ounces plain Greek yogurt (I like Fage brand)

½ garlic clove, minced

½ cup loosely packed fresh dill, roughly chopped

1 tablespoon fresh lemon juice

¼ teaspoon agave nectar

Maldon or other flaky salt to taste

Freshly ground black pepper to taste

Mix all the ingredients together in a glass bowl, cover, and refrigerate. Serve chilled.

hot! mexican salsa

{ Makes about 4 cups }

Buying condiments is tempting, I know. We're all busy and often concentrate our efforts on the main components of a dish, but this is a great example of a condiment that's worth it, because it's incredibly low maintenance and easy to make, and it has a wonderful deep smoky flavor from the blackened skins.

You can keep it in a mason jar in the refrigerator for a week or so. If you don't have tomatillos or can't find them, no worries, just use more tomatoes.

4 whole tomatoes

2 tomatillos

1 whole jalapeño chile

3 unpeeled garlic cloves

Maldon or other flaky salt

Agave nectar

Squeeze of lime

1. Preheat the broiler.

2. Place the tomatoes, tomatillos, jalapeño, and garlic on a baking sheet on the top shelf of the oven under the broiler. Place the tomatoes and tomatillos upside down so that the greatest amount of surface area is exposed to the broiler.

3. Broil the vegetables for about 10 minutes, until the skin is blackened. (Remove the garlic after 5 to 7 minutes—the garlic shouldn't be black, just roasted. Peel the garlic.) See the pictures for Blackened Tomato Soup (page 46)—you really want the skin of the tomatoes, tomatillos, and jalapeño to be black to get a smoky flavor.

4. Remove the tomatoes, tomatillos, and jalapeño from the oven and place in a blender with the roasted garlic. Puree until it's a chunky consistency. Season with salt, agave, and lime juice. Check the seasoning again before serving.

hummus

{ Makes about 1 cup }

Making your own hummus is a satisfying task—so quick, and it's going to taste so much better than anything you'll find in a grocery store.

One 15-ounce can chickpeas

1 or 2 garlic cloves, minced

1½ teaspoons ground cumin

¼ cup tahini

Maldon or other flaky salt

Freshly ground black pepper

½ lemon

1. Drain about two-thirds of the liquid from the chickpea can and reserve the rest.

2. Add the chickpeas and their reserved juices to a food processor. Add the garlic, cumin, and tahini and pulse until combined. Season with salt and pepper and add a good squeeze of lemon. Pulse again, taste, and adjust the seasonings.

NOTE: *It's your choice how smooth you make the hummus. I don't like mine to be too smooth, but go with what you like. The most important thing is that you like the way it tastes, so make sure the seasoning makes you happy and add more lemon if you like.*

pineapple and chile relish

{ Makes about 2 cups }

This isn't exactly a traditional South African condiment, but it definitely feels like something I'd be served in South Africa. I've served it alongside Cape Malay Lamb Curry (page 183), but it would also work well with a barbecued lamb or pork chop or any Indian curry.

2 cups finely diced pineapple

1½ teaspoons minced fresh ginger

½ tablespoon minced red onion

Zest of 1 lime

½ serrano chile, seeds and all, minced

1 pinch Maldon or other flaky salt

¼ cup agave nectar

1 small handful fresh cilantro leaves, chopped

1 small handful fresh mint leaves, chopped, optional

1. Put the pineapple, ginger, onion, lime zest, chile, salt, and agave nectar in a saucepan along with 1½ cups water. Bring to a simmer over low heat and simmer for 35 to 40 minutes, until pretty much all of the liquid has cooked away.

2. Let the mixture cool, then add the cilantro and, if you wish, mint leaves.

nut salad dressing

{ Makes ¼ cup }

A salad dressing made out of a nut oil adds a certain richness to a dish. I've used this on the Trout, Pear, and Mâche Salad (page 107), but I also like it as a vinaigrette for some cooked dishes. For example, if you roast some cauliflower with a few mustard seeds and serve it with a piece of pan-seared sea bass, this would be a lovely dressing to drizzle on top. You can substitute any nut oil you like.

1 tablespoon good-quality nut oil (I use hazelnut oil, but walnut is good too)

1 teaspoon agave nectar

½ garlic clove, minced

1 teaspoon Dijon mustard

½ tablespoon fresh lemon juice

1 pinch Maldon or other flaky salt

Freshly ground black pepper to taste

1. Place all the ingredients in a mason jar or small covered plastic container and shake!

2. Taste for seasoning and refrigerate until ready to use.

sesame and lemon dipping sauce

{ Makes a little more than ½ cup }

Tahini is basically just ground sesame seeds, and is often used in North African, Greek, and Turkish cooking. It's really smooth and tastes so rich, but it's wonderfully good for you—it's high in antioxidants and is said to lower your blood pressure. This tahini-based sauce is really versatile and awesome paired with Chickpea and Corn Falafel (page 235) or Lamb and Quinoa Koftas (page 219). Or add more water to turn it into a salad dressing.

1½ tablespoons sesame seeds

¼ cup tahini

2 teaspoons fresh lemon juice

Maldon or other flaky salt to taste

Freshly ground black pepper to taste

2 teaspoons agave nectar

1. Toast the sesame seeds in a small dry skillet over medium heat. This'll only take about a minute. Keep a close eye on them—they can burn really quickly!

2. Place all the ingredients in a bowl and mix. Use a fork to whisk in 3 tablespoons water to make a sauce. Beautiful!

tomato sauce

{ Makes about 2 cups }

This beautiful, rustic tomato sauce is a favorite of DVF's. My friend Anne asked me for a tomato pasta recipe years ago when we worked together, but she requested that I make it with ginger. I didn't really like the sound of it at first but made it for her anyway. Needless to say, I loved the tomato and ginger combination—it's really interesting.

I like this versatile sauce with Poached Salmon with Shrimp Served on Couscous (page 161), or with shrimp or barbecued chicken. It's a great thing to have in the fridge, so you might as well make a double batch, or more.

2 tablespoons extra virgin olive oil	Maldon or other flaky salt
½ red onion, finely chopped	Freshly ground black pepper
2 garlic cloves, minced	1 lemon
2 tablespoons minced fresh ginger	Agave nectar
2 cups cherry tomatoes	

1. Heat the olive oil in a saucepan over low heat. Add the onion, garlic, and ginger and sweat, cooking for at least 8 minutes—don't rush it. The onion should be very soft, translucent, and sweet.

2. Add the tomatoes and season with salt and pepper. Keep the heat low and cook them down for another 30 minutes. Stir the mixture occasionally, taking care that it doesn't burn, and add a touch more oil if you like. When the skin of the tomatoes starts to break, squash some of the tomatoes with the back of a fork.

3. To finish off the sauce, give it a small squeeze of lemon juice and a bit of agave nectar. Taste and adjust the seasoning if necessary.

guacamole

{ Makes 3 to 4 cups }

I know you've probably made guacamole before, but I really think you should give this recipe a try. Guacamole is good, but add ginger and it becomes incredible! Really, give it a go. It's so quick and easy, and totally worth the effort. It'll be the first thing gone from the table.

4 ripe avocados, peeled, pitted, and cubed

1 heaping tablespoon minced fresh ginger

2 garlic cloves, minced

1 squeeze agave nectar

½ red chile (preferably serrano), seeded and chopped

Juice of 2 limes

1 large handful fresh cilantro leaves and stems, roughly chopped

Maldon or other flaky salt to taste

Freshly ground black pepper to taste

Place all the ingredients in a blender. Blend until slightly chunky, or as smooth as you'd like. Adjust the seasoning as needed.

tomato pesto

{ Makes about 2 cups }

It's good to have some basic sauce recipes that you can pull out at any time to take something to the next level, and this is one of them. You could serve this on top of a quick grilled steak, under a beautiful piece of grilled fish, or tossed through some pasta. I love it with the Green Herb and Lemon Zest Gnocchi (page 136).

Let's quickly address the anchovies—I love them, but many people don't. I think they get a pretty bad rap, though . . . they have the ability to add so much depth to a simple dish or sauce like this one, and they leave no "fishy" taste at all.

⅓ cup pine nuts

2 large vine-ripened tomatoes, roughly chopped

1 garlic clove, minced

2 anchovy fillets, roughly chopped

¾ cup grated Parmesan

1 teaspoon extra virgin olive oil

Squeeze of agave nectar

1 small handful fresh mint leaves, roughly chopped

1 small handful fresh basil leaves, roughly chopped

Squeeze of lemon juice

Maldon or other flaky salt

Freshly ground black pepper

1. In a small dry skillet, toast the pine nuts until golden, stirring often, about 2 minutes.

2. Put all the ingredients into a blender and blend until you reach the consistency you like. I like it quite chunky, but some people prefer it smoother—up to you.

   NOTE: *The pesto will keep in the fridge for a couple of days. It will separate a bit, but no worries—just give it a quick mix and it'll come together really easily.*

A beautiful boy in the Solomon Islands. I bought fifteen of these old Coca-Cola bottles from him. They'd been hand-dived from a World War II wreck. Amazing!

Acknowledgments

I've always been taken such good care of. All over the world, I've met kind, generous people who have looked after me, had me in their homes and around their table, and made me feel welcome. Traveling has been a wonderful way to see that the world is bursting with good people.

I've been equally lucky regarding this book, and I give my deepest thanks to those who have helped:

Diane von Furstenberg. Where do I start? There truly isn't enough space to write all the ways in which you've been so incredibly generous and supportive, and so I hope you believe me when I say that I'm grateful for *every. single. thing.* And always will be. Mr. Diller: thank you.

My little photography team: John Bedell, Allegra Hsiao, and Janell Hughes. We did it. I really couldn't have worked with better people for this. John—amazing talent + passion + hard work = greatness. The photos are beautiful. Thank you so much. Thanks, Allie, for your effortless style and impeccable taste, and for always finding a way to make me smile. And Janell—you were the perfect fit into this little photo quartet. Thank you for your patience and assistance with everything.

Tatiana von Furstenberg, one of the funniest people I've met, and also incredibly generous. Thank you for giving me an amazing place to hide out in New York City, and for looking after me in L.A. You're the best. Thank you.

Thank you so much, Alex von Furstenberg and Ali Kay, for opening your home and giving me a spectacular space to stay and be inspired. Your home was where I gathered my thoughts, and took big steps, and I appreciate it so much. And to Talita and Tassilo for allowing me to use your wonderful kitchen for some of the photos.

AK, for the introduction to the amazing Andrea Rosen! Andrea, I have so much appreciation for you, it's crazy—you were so supportive from the very beginning, and I can't tell you how much that meant and still means to me. And for all the ongoing help: invaluable. You rule. (Really.) Thank you.

The William Morrow people are all wonderful, really. Kara Zauberman—thank you for all your hard work, and to everyone else that I've worked with and am looking forward to working with: Liate Stehlik, Lynn Grady, Tavia Kowalchuk, Megan Swartz, Katie Steinberg, Joyce Wong, and Karen Lumley. Thank you, Mary Schuck, for the beautiful cover, and Lorie Pagnozzi, for the freshest, happiest, most beautiful interior design. I genuinely feel so lucky to be working with this group of people.

It's so cool that I get to refer to someone as "my editor," and then to actually get the best one in the business is crazy. Cassie Jones, you're as sharp as my chef's knife. I have so much respect—thank you for your patience, support, and for guiding me so, so well.

I was a little overwhelmed when I flew into busy New York for the first time from the quiet Pacific, and so thank you, Ellen Gross, for keeping an eye out for me, and letting me come over and eat chicken soup in a great home environment. Thank you also for the ongoing support and understanding.

When it was time for me to be in Connecticut, the setting couldn't have been more perfect—thank you, Lourdes Mecha, for taking such good care of me at the beautifully serene Cloudwalk.

Genevieve Ernst—you've been the hugest help, and I appreciate all of it. Your enthusiasm and encouragement has meant a lot. Thank you so much.

Sarah Knutson, you've gone above and beyond to help me out—thank you, thank you. As a colleague and a person, I have the hugest respect.

Luisella Meloni—we're just starting to work on some things together now, and judging by how great you've been so far in such a short period of time, I know I will want to extend a massive thank-you by the time this prints. I love working with you.

Rebecca Szczypka—thank you for being my little rock. Your support has always been immeasurable and invaluable.

Shout-out to my little *Eos* family! We've traveled around the world together, worked hard, and made some of the most amazing memories and tight bonds. Thanks especially to Hannah Zarnack, for always being there and making my life better.

Ambassador Hall—for being my first mentor and giving me amazing opportunities.

David Higgs—for teaching me to cook and making it so easy to fall in love with food.

Finally, to my mom and dad—thank you for introducing me to travel at such a young age, and for always making us sit around a table. I love you, and I'm so lucky you're my parents.

Index

Note: Page references in *italics* indicate recipe photographs.

Vanuatu

Solomon Islands